The

SEVEN YEARS IN TIBET
Screenplay and Story Behind the Film

The
SEVEN YEARS IN TIBET
Screenplay and Story Behind the Film

by Jean-Jacques Annaud, Becky Johnston, and Laurence B. Chollet

Screenplay by Becky Johnston

Foreword by Jetsun Pema
Afterword by Robert A. F. Thurman

Photographs by
Jean-Jacques Annaud, David Appleby, Pat Morrow, and Bill Kaye
with historical photographs by Heinrich Harrer

Edited by Alisa Tager

A NEWMARKET PICTORIAL MOVIEBOOK

Newmarket Press • New York

10 9 8 7 6 5 4 3 2 1

Library of Congress Cataloging-in-Publication Data

Johnston, Becky, 1955-
    The Seven Years in Tibet screenplay and story behind the film / Jean-Jacques Annaud, Becky Johnston, Laurence B. Chollet.
        p. cm. — (Newmarket pictorial moviebook)
    Includes bibliographical references.
    ISBN 1-55704-342-6 (hardcover)
    I. Seven years in Tibet (Motion picture)
2. Annaud, Jean-Jacques. I. Chollet, Laurence B.
II. Title. III. Series.
PN1997.S375J65 1997
791.43'72—DC21   97-29129
                                CIP

Quantity Purchases

Companies, professional groups, clubs, and other organizations may qualify for special terms when ordering quantities of this title.

For information, write Special Sales, Newmarket Press, 18 East 48th Street, New York, NY 10017, call (212) 832-3575, or FAX (212) 832-3629.

Produced by Newmarket Productions, a division of Newmarket Publishing & Communications Company: Esther Margolis, director; Keith Hollaman, editor; Joe Gannon, production manager; Rachel Reiss, assistant editor; Marilyn Kretzer, rights manager.

Editorial, design, and production services by Walking Stick Press, San Francisco: Diana Landau, editor; Linda Herman, book design; Miriam Lewis and Joanna Lynch, design associates.

Manufactured in the United States of America

Other Newmarket Pictorial Moviebooks include:
Men in Black: The Script and Story Behind the Film
Dances With Wolves: The Illustrated Story of the Epic Film
Bram Stoker's Dracula: The Film and the Legend
Mary Shelley's Frankenstein: The Classic Tale of Terror Reborn on Film
The Sense and Sensibility Screenplay & Diaries
The Age of Innocence: A Portrait of the Film Based on the Novel by Edith Wharton
City of Joy: The Illustrated Story of the Film
Wyatt Earp: The Film and the Filmmakers
Panther: A Pictorial History of the Black Panthers and the Story Behind the Film
Showgirls: Portrait of the Film

Newmarket Shooting Scripts™ include:
Ice Storm: The Shooting Script
Dead Man Walking: The Shooting Script
The Birdcage: The Shooting Script
The Shawshank Redemption: The Shooting Script
The People vs. Larry Flynt: The Shooting Script
The Age of Innocence: The Shooting Script
Swept from the Sea: The Shooting Script
U-Turn: The Shooting Script

CONTENTS

Map of Tibet and Heinrich Harrer's Route   6

FOREWORD
Rediscovering Lost Tibet
by Jetsun Pema   8

PREFACE
A Metamorphosis of the Soul
by Jean-Jacques Annaud   12

Quest for Heart
by Laurence B. Chollet   14

The Screenplay
by Becky Johnston   72

AFTERWORD
Screening the Truth about Tibet
by Professor Robert A. F. Thurman   216

Further Reading   220

Film Credits   222

About the Authors   223

Acknowledgments   224

Heavy line shows author's itinerary.

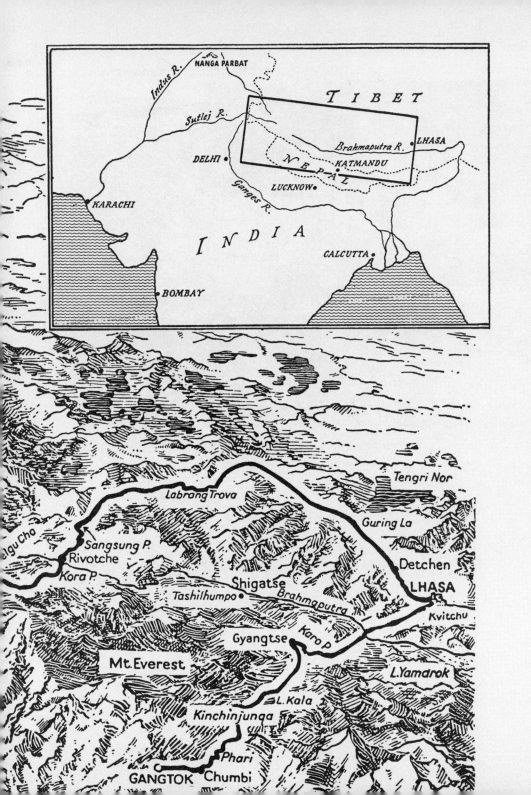

The family of the Dalai Lama including, front row, left to right, the Dalai Lama's nephew, his elder sister Tsering Doma, his mother, and his younger sister Jetsun Pema. The others are family attendants. Historical photograph by Heinrich Harrer.

Rediscovering Lost Tibet

by Jetsun Pema
Sister of His Holiness the Fourteenth Dalai Lama

Although Tibetans live scattered in small communities throughout India, news travels really fast. The news of two proposed Hollywood movies about Tibet spread like wildfire among the world's estimated 130,000 Tibetan exiles. Everyone was talking about it and asking all sorts of questions.

So when the casting director for *Seven Years in Tibet* came to see me, I already knew quite a bit about what was happening. She asked me if I would like to meet Jean-Jacques Annaud, the director of the movie, when he came to Delhi, to which I agreed.

We met in Delhi some time later. Jean-Jacques asked me to act in the movie, and I told him that I would first like to see the script and a film he had previously directed. I saw *The Bear* and was deeply moved by it. It has a wonderful connection with Buddhism and Buddhism's primary concern of generating compassion. I felt that a person who made such a movie as *The Bear* would make a movie on Tibet with the same sensitivity.

I thought a lot about *Seven Years in Tibet* and my own role in it. My children and relatives urged me to take up the offer, since they could not picture anyone else acting the part of my mother. So when I met Jean-Jacques again, I told him I would take part.

Acting in the movie was an unforgettable experience for all the Tibetans who were involved. Old and young alike, we came to learn a great deal about Tibet in the 1940s. The older people relived our country's recent past, and some even reenacted their own roles in shaping the very events that engulfed Tibet. For the young, it was a moving discovery of a homeland they had heard about, and a real eye-opener to our country's rich traditions and wonderful culture. Many of them had hardly believed that Tibet was such a place as the movie portrayed, and their curiosity about and enthusiasm for the cause of Tibet's freedom increased manyfold.

To all of us, the movie became an eloquent voice for the anguish of Tibet.

Seven Years in Tibet tells the story of Heinrich Harrer and Peter Aufschnaiter, two Austrian mountaineers who escaped British internment in India and managed to escape to Tibet, where the people welcomed them as friends. The movie ends when the forces of communist China rumbled into Tibet, smashing up the culture and love of life of the peace-loving Tibetans. It was then that Harrer made up his mind to leave, after spending seven wonderful years in the country.

The time when Harrer left Tibet was also the time when the Tibetans' peaceful existence came to a tragic end. Having believed for centuries that the world would leave it alone, Tibet was not equipped to defend itself when China marched in. In the end, the Tibet seen through the eyes of Harrer, the Tibet of the 1940s, the Tibet that inspired the myth and dream of Shangri-La, was lost forever. The old Tibet has indeed become a "lost horizon."

People of more than twenty-five different nationalities from across the world took part in the making of *Seven Years in Tibet*. We literally took over the little town of Uspallata in the Argentinean Andes. Everyone was so friendly and it was so peaceful up there—just like old Tibet. It was also a wonderful reunion for the Tibetans. Since going into exile, they had settled in different countries, and this was the first time they had the opportunity to meet again.

The driving force behind this enormous effort was the director himself. Jean-Jacques Annaud worked hard from early morning to late at night, seven days a week. It was encouraging to see that he believed in the capacity of every one of us to contribute our very best towards making his movie. The whole unit, the cast and crew, worked so effectively and harmoniously, and we all became one big family.

The re-creations on the different sets of the Potala steps, the Jokhang, and the Lhasa streets deeply affected all the Tibetans. We saw these icons of the Tibetan identity and knew that the originals were no more. For me personally, to relive the Tibet of my childhood and to act the role of my own mother was a wonderful and moving experience. Many times, tears came to my eyes, and I had to tell myself that this was "only a movie." It was hard but I managed.

Being part of *Seven Years in Tibet* made us all the more aware that our beautiful country is now no more. The movie was like a dream that we wanted never to end, and we hope that someday this dream will come true.

A Metamorphosis of the Soul

by Jean-Jacques Annaud

One fear haunted my childhood: that of resembling my father. Two key events marked my transition from childhood to adulthood: the revelation that my father was not my father, and the discovery of Africa, which enabled me to discover my inner jungle. My films all revolve, more or less, around this fear and these two shocks.

My first film, *Black and White in Color*, tells the story of a young French intellectual who is transformed by his contact with the African continent. Twenty years and eight films later, *Seven Years in Tibet* shows the metamorphosis of a young, egocentric, opportunistic Austrian into an endearing human being, thanks to his lengthy immersion in a culture vastly different from ours and his, and his exposure to people who conduct themselves by a completely different value system.

Can knowledge, enlightenment, or efforts to improve oneself create the opportunity to amend what heredity dictates, as I once hoped so strongly as a child? Can culture alter nature? Can reason triumph over instinct? My Neanderthal hero of *Quest For Fire* becomes more human after encountering a tribe more advanced than his own. His journey of initiation improves him, as does the journey undertaken by my young mammal protagonist in *The Bear*. The bear also encounters another tribe with curious manners—that of men—and the two plantigrade species are enriched by their mutual differences.

My fascination with books, and the corresponding hope that knowledge brings, are at the heart of *The Name of the Rose*. I brought together the elements of this bountiful novel through the story of the apprenticeship of a young man, a novice who discovers the reality behind the appearance of a monastery dedicated to learning: a world where the wild nature of instinct triumphs over the reassuring luxuries of culture.

In *The Lover*, Asia, not Africa, becomes the developing bath for a similar picture. There, the delicate mammal in the process of development is a young white girl who discovers herself in the steamy air of a Saigon bachelor pad, pressed against the loins of a Chinese man. Later, she will become one of the most respected intellectuals of her time, enriched by her cultural cross-pollination, nourished by the blended silt of the Mekong and the Seine.

I try to change the masks and costumes to give the illusion that I am not always repeating the same text. But in all these disguises, I am the same worried little boy, still looking for answers to the same questions. I hope that you will forgive him for once again making the same film.

QUEST FOR HEART

Jean-Jacques Annaud and the Filming of *Seven Years in Tibet*

by *Laurence B. Chollet*

Jean-Jacques Annaud has made his reputation as an offbeat filmmaker with such creations as *Quest For Fire*, *The Name of The Rose*, and *The Bear*, and this has given him an a certain cachet in Hollywood.

He's the director who gets flooded with odd stories that nobody knows quite what to do with. Horse stories, woman pirate stories, epics about the Spanish Conquistadors, and film bios on unusual folks like legendary war photographer Robert Capa: all manage to find their way to Annaud. So it wasn't surprising that three years ago a script about a mountain climber reached Annaud's desk.

"One day an agent from ICM came to me with a script and said, 'You should read this. It's something that you should be interested in.' And I read a very bad screenplay based on the true story of the mountain climber Heinrich Harrer, who escaped into Tibet and became the Dalai Lama's first foreign friend," Annaud recalls. "I was intrigued by the framework of the story, so I bought the book, read it, and was still intrigued. Something was missing. The writer talked about the blisters on his feet—but he never talked about the blisters on his heart.... And I wanted to find them."

Annaud found those "blisters" and much more, and the results can be seen in *Seven Years In Tibet*, starring Brad Pitt, David Thewlis, and an international cast that includes some 150 Tibetans. Among those is Jetsun Pema, sister of His Holiness the fourteenth Dalai Lama; she plays the role of their mother.

The film is based on a period in the life of Harrer, the legendary Austrian climber who set out to scale Nanga Parbat in 1939, was interned in a British prisoner-of-war camp in India, then escaped into Tibet, where he stayed seven years and became the first Western tutor—and friend—of the young Dalai Lama. It's an epic story that traces the spiritual redemption of Harrer (played by Pitt), who, aided by his friend and fellow climber, Peter Aufschnaiter (Thewlis), found a new life through Tibetan Buddhism.

It's also a tale right up Annaud's alley. He prides himself on making films in remote locales, under extreme conditions, and is obsessed with stories about people emotionally transformed by their contact with nature or other cultures. It's a recurrent theme in his films—from his first, *Black and White in Color*, set in colonial West Africa during World War I, to his most recent, *Wings of Courage*, an IMAX 3-D feature about the legendary French aviator Henri Guillaumet, who crashed his plane in the Andes and walked out to safety.

To explore these conflicts, Annaud loves to immerse himself in the subject matter he is filming, then build entire worlds from the ground up, using the best technicians and craftsmen he can find. But this time out, the challenge was ambitious, even for Annaud. For all intents and purposes, Tibet has been a closed country to Western eyes for centuries. Harrer and Aufschnaiter, in fact, were among the few Westerners ever permitted to live in Lhasa, the so-called "Forbidden City" of Tibet. As a result, there exist only a handful of firsthand, accurate Western accounts of Tibet, and only a limited amount of other material on the country is available.

The spread of knowledge hasn't been helped by the Chinese. China invaded Tibet in 1949 and has since ruled the ancient kingdom like a conquered province, forcing the Dalai Lama and many of his followers to flee the country in 1959.

Consequently, filming in Tibet was impossible, so Annaud set his sights on northern India. In early 1996 he spent several months and some $3 million scouting locations and preparing sets, only to have his plans dashed at the last moment when in April the Indian government—reportedly under pressure from China—refused him official permission to film. Undeterred, Annaud moved his production halfway around the globe to western Argentina and the high plateaus of the Andes. There he began to build his own "Tibet."

"Our goal is twofold," Annaud says. "One is to make a very good, entertaining movie. The other is to make a movie that is going to be one of the few to witness the culture of Tibet as it was."

To Film a Hidden World

In some ways, Harrer's story is the stuff of Hollywood dreams. It has great visuals, a dramatic story, and a real-world angle: Harrer, after all, didn't become friends with just anyone, but with the Dalai Lama, arguably the best-known spiritual leader in the world and winner of the Nobel Prize for Peace in 1989 for his nonviolent campaign against Chinese rule in Tibet.

A good deal of the story's appeal has to do with Tibet itself, the so-called "Land of Snows," which was shut off from Western eyes for centuries. That was in large part because of its location: the 471,700-square-mile country—an area about the size of Western Europe—is situated on a high plateau, some 16,000 feet above sea level. It's bordered on the south by the Himalayas and Mount Everest (29,028 feet high) and on the north by the Kunlun Range, which rises some 20,000 feet.

Those mountains posed a natural barrier to the outside world, and Tibet's isolation was enhanced by the Buddhist religion. Buddhism was introduced from India in the seventh century, and by the seventeenth century the country was virtually a theocracy, headed by a spiritual and political leader called the Dalai Lama.

The position was not elected but passed on through reincarnation. Tibetan Buddhists believe there is only one Dalai Lama and he is reborn continually. Historically, when a reigning Dalai Lama died, a contingent of monks searched the country looking for his reincarnation in a young boy. Once found, the boy was taken to Lhasa and trained by monks until he reached his majority and could be crowned "Dalai Lama." (The current Dalai Lama—the fourteenth Dalai Lama, Tenzin Gyatso—was born in

Circa 1950 photograph taken by Heinrich Harrer, of a three-year-old Tibetan boy, Drigung Rinpoche, who has been recognized as an incarnate lama, leaving his grandparents' home to be educated at a monastery. Harrer's historical photos appear occasionally in this chapter.

1935 and discovered in 1938 in the small farming village of Takster in the Amdo region of Tibet.)

The Dalai Lama's power was consolidated by large numbers of monks. Up to 20 percent of the male population, at times, belonged to one of the many Buddhist orders. Virtually every town had its own monastery called a "lamasery," which trained its monks in meditation and sacred arts such as creating *mandalas*—intricate sand paintings made from finely crushed stones. As such, the monasteries (many of which had a private army) served as the spiritual, intellectual, and political centers of their local communities.

Tibetan Buddhist monks living in exile portray themselves in the film. Here they create a man- *dala. All photos in this chapter, except the historical photographs by Heinrich Harrer so identified, are from the production of* Seven Years in Tibet.

The Gelupga order wielded enormous power within the Tibetan government. It controlled the huge monastic complexes of Dreprung and Sera in the capital city of Lhasa, and fiercely sought to maintain the religious state by shunning modernization and restricting outside visitors.

As a result, Tibet remained a closed, mysterious country. Few Westerners set foot in the country, let alone stayed, until the British set up a trade mission in Lhasa in 1904.

But all that began to change in 1950, when the Chinese Communists, asserting a historical right to Tibet, invaded the country and forced Tibet to sign an agreement surrendering its sovereignty. Technically, the agreement allowed the Dalai Lama to rule and ensured religious freedom. But in

Several well-known Asian actors play featured roles as Tibetans in the film. Here, the minister Kungo Tsarong, played by the Japanese actor Mako, flees Lhasa along with other Tibetans after the Chinese invasion.

reality, the Chinese ruthlessly tightened their control on the country during the 1950s, and in 1959 forced the Dalai Lama and members of his cabinet to flee to northern India, where they set up a government in exile in Dharamsala. Some 80,000 Tibetans followed, and now more than 100,000 live in settlements in India, Nepal, Bhutan, and Sikkim and recognize the Dalai Lama as their leader.

For nearly two decades, Tibet was again off limits to foreigners, as the Chinese carried out a vicious repression of Buddhist culture. They conducted a systematic campaign of genocide and mass destruction of monastic towns. The holy city of Lhasa, for instance, has only 2 percent of the typical Tibetan houses left. The Chinese divided Tibet into one so-called Autonomous Region (home to about one-third of all Tibetans), one separate province (Qinghai), and four autonomous prefectures of other Chinese provinces.

It was only in the late 1980s that the Chinese began to rebuild and reopen some famous shrines and monasteries to lure Western tourists. But even now, large sections of the country, particularly in the remote northern regions along the Chinese border, are off limits to westerners.

The Tale of a Man Reborn

Adding to Tibet's historical drama was Harrer's own story. In 1938, he was part of the first team to scale the deadly north face of the Eiger (some 6,000 feet of sheer ice) in the Swiss Alps. That gave him the chance to try Nanga Parbat, a 25,000-foot peak in the Himalayas.

He never made the summit because World War II broke out, and he was captured by the British while climbing and was interned, along with team leader Peter Aufschnaiter and two other companions. His escape and subsequent trek with Aufschnaiter from India into Tibet—they climbed for two years, through some thirty mountain passes between 15,000 and 20,000 feet—is considered one of the greatest mountaineering feats on record. That they made it through such extremely high altitudes without the aid of modern climbing devices as oxygen tanks and high-tech gear is simply mind-boggling.

Harrer's climbing achievements made him a German folk hero of the 1930s: he was nationally feted, photographed with Adolf Hitler, and given an honorary position in the SS as a sports trainer, with a rank equivalent to sergeant. He shamelessly put his connections to work furthering his climbing career.

"I joined the Nazi organizations because I wanted to climb," the

The real Heinrich Harrer, shown with his servant in this archival photo, sits on the flank of 23,996-foot Chomo Lhari, a sacred peak on the Tibet-Bhutan border.

eighty-five-year-old Harrer would later explain, when revelations about his Nazi past came to light in the summer of 1997. "If I had not been a member, I would not have been able to take part in the Nanga Parbat [expedition] in 1939."

Harrer's ruthless egocentricity was radically changed by seven years in Tibet. His contact with Buddhism, with the young Dalai Lama (who was just fifteen when they met in 1950), and with a culture that is not success-driven in the Western sense would lead him into another way of thinking and doing. He was changed by those experiences—and, undoubtedly, by the destruction of Germany in the war—and became a tireless advocate of the Tibetan cause, human rights, nonviolence, and racial equality by the time he fled the country in 1951 in the wake of the Chinese invasion.

"The daily life of Tibetans is ordered by religious belief," Harrer wrote in his memoir, *Seven Years in Tibet* (1953), which has sold millions of copies worldwide. "Pious texts are constantly on their lips; prayer wheels turn without ceasing; the rain, the wind, all the phenomena of nature bear witness to the universal presence of the gods.

"Prayer lamps burn everywhere, in the house of the noble and the tent of the nomad," he continued. "Earthly existence is of little worth in Tibet and death has no terrors.

"One cannot close one's heart to the religious fervor that radiates from everyone," he added. "Even after a short time in the country, it was no longer possible for one thoughtlessly to kill a fly."

But despite the inherent drama in Harrer's story, the project eluded capture in script and on screen for decades. A good deal of the trouble was simply that there was not one story but many stories in Harrer's tale. And finding a dramatic structure that covered all the bases coherently had baffled more than one screenwriter.

Heinrich Harrer photographed a group of his Tibetan friends outside the Western-style home he built for himself in Lhasa.

A Passion for the Exotic

The fifty-three-year-old Annaud is no stranger to such challenges—indeed, he has built his career on them. Born and raised in Draveil, a working-class suburb of Paris, the only child of a professional secretary and a railroad worker, he developed a love of film from trips to the local cinema on Sundays with his parents.

By age six, Annaud had his own camera—a Brownie Kodak box. By eleven he had made his first documentary with his first 8mm camera: a short film on France's medieval churches, which he visited with his parents on summer vacations. By nineteen, he had graduated first in his class from the Vaugirard School in Paris, the country's leading technical film school. Two years later, he had earned his film degree from the prestigious IDHEC (Institut des Hautes Etudes Cinématographiques)—and simultaneously earned a B.A. from the Sorbonne, where he majored in theater, Greek, and the history and art of the Middle Ages. By twenty-one, he was directing commercials; by twenty-seven, he was one of the leading commercial directors in Europe, with more than 500 commercials under his belt.

His passion for foreign places was discovered by accident. He had just graduated from film school at twenty-one, and was getting a lot of work as a commercial director, when he was conscripted into the French army and sent to West Africa. The prospect of two years abroad filled him with loathing, as he considered Africa to be nothing but "a lot of black people beating tom-toms." But that changed when he stepped off the plane and was hit with a blast of tropical heat carrying the smells of a mysterious culture.

"When the door to the plane opened, I just fell apart," Annaud recalls. "I just loved it—the smell of rotten fruit, the humidity, the rain forest. . . . I had no chance! They were speaking another language, it was another civilization there. And after two or three days, I never had such a great time. I knew I could relate to those people because it was there I discovered that I could have emotions. Up until that time, I had been very synthetic—I had only valued the intellect. Anything coming from my guts I did not like. . . . Africa taught me differently."

Annaud's experiences in Africa set the stage for what would become his passion for traveling to foreign lands and studying their cultures. It also gave him recurrent themes to explore in his films.

His first feature, *Black and White in Color,* was set in West Africa and won the Oscar for Best Foreign Film in 1977. It told the story of a young French colonial who was transformed by his experience during World War I. *Quest for Fire* dealt with one primitive man's discovery of fire through his contact with a more advanced prehistoric tribe. *The Name of the Rose* explored a young Austrian monk's discovery of passion, love, and death in a medieval monastery, while *The Lover* focused on a French girl's coming of age in the arms of an older Chinese man in 1920s French Indochina.

Seen in relation to these films, *Seven Years* clearly had all the elements of an "Annaud drama" and more. Harrer's story, as Annaud likes to say, was one he could personally identify with.

A major turning point in Annaud's life arrived when he was twenty-nine. He had become one of the best-known commercial directors in Europe, earned a pile of money, a wall full of awards, bought a farm in the Loiret, and was miserable. He had achieved "success" but at the expense of his self-respect: he was tied to making commercials about some products he didn't believe in and others that were downright deadly. Once, he made a series of award-winning commercials for a brand of rain tires, demonstrating how safe they were; the tires, it turned out, were defective, wound up causing hundreds of accidents, and were eventually banned.

Experiences like that ultimately led Annaud to suffer a nervous collapse. He quit the commercial business and sought his personal salvation in making the kind of movies that first drew him as a young boy to the cinema: those that involved the human heart in conflict with itself. Annaud's experiences in the world of commercials also gave him an understanding of the darker side of himself and of human nature: how the relentless drive for success, money, power, fame, and material possessions—all the things Western culture holds dear—can pave the way to a personal hell from which there may be no escape.

And he saw in Harrer's story a unique chance to explore these dark regions of the heart. It is a story about a man who made a Faustian bargain to further his fame and career, then wound up in Tibet, where all his material possessions—including his fame—were stripped away, and he was forced to confront the person he never met: himself.

Much of that self-confrontation was painful. Harrer came to regret very deeply that he subscribed to antisemitic propaganda as part of his

National Socialist activities. After his experiences in Tibet, he called his prewar antisemitism "the great shame of my life." That shame—and the abiding guilt that surrounded it—undoubtedly spurred Harrer's later dedication to human rights.

Needless to say, this kind of moral complexity generally sends most Hollywood filmmakers running for cover—or a good rewrite man, to chop the story down into black-and-white characters, a clever narrative, and a happy ending. But for Annaud, the complexity of Harrer's story made it all the more challenging to capture on film: the more complexities, the better. Harrer's story was remarkable: the depth of his conceit and immoral ambition was outdone only by the magnitude of his personal transformation.

"It's the whole story of this film," Annaud says. "This man, Harrer, is a man who leaves his country very famous and very unhappy. And returns with no possessions but himself—and eventually winds up very, very ashamed of what he had been.

"This is why Brad wanted to the do the movie, instinctively, because this theme appeals to him," Annaud notes. "I know Brad doesn't want to have ten houses—he wants to be a respected actor, although he'd never say a thing like that. . . . Instead of a rich person, he wants to be a good man.

"And if you ask me why I wanted to do this movie, the reason is the same: because of that theme," Annaud adds. "In many movies the theme itself is about making money: the treasure to find, the safe to break open, the fat check to reach. A great number of films are 'about' a guy who wants to become the champion of something. By the end of the film, he makes it—and gets the gold.

"We start where most movies end," Annaud observes. "Harrer is a champion. Rich, famous, and unhappy. And we ask the question, 'Why?'"

From Memoir to Screenplay

No sooner had Annaud made up his mind to explore Harrer's story than TriStar Pictures executive Michael Besman suggested that he talk with a screenwriter named Becky Johnston. She was very interested in Buddhism.

Born and raised in Michigan, Johnston was trained as a fine arts painter at Rhode Island School of Design and Brown University, then did a stint in the downtown art world of lower Manhattan in the early 1980s before striking out west with a desire to write films. She moved to Los Angeles, supported herself through a variety of part-time jobs, and spent as much time she could at the American Film Institute Library, teaching herself to write scripts. She broke through with a feature script for Prince entitled *Under the Cherry Moon,* then hit it big with *The Prince of Tides,* a script she co-wrote with novelist Pat Conroy. It was nominated for an Academy Award in 1991.

Johnston and Annaud immediately hit it off and discovered they saw eye-to-eye on a major point.

"From our first meeting," Johnston said, "Jean-Jacques and I realized that what this story was about, at heart, was two lonely people [Harrer and the young Dalai Lama] who meet and find each other."

To prepare for writing the story, Johnston immersed herself in Buddhism, studying with a Tibetan lama in Los Angeles for months, then touring Tibet in a small group with noted Buddhist scholar Stephen Batchelor. She eventually found her way to Dharamsala, India, where she lived for a month and conducted extensive interviews with just about everyone she could find who was connected to the Dalai Lama—including His Holiness himself. These travels not only gave her a deeper understanding of Buddhism and Tibet, but provided a big clue about what had been missing from Harrer's book.

Heinrich Harrer, with his back to the camera, on a visit to the Gyantse monastery, once a major monastic center containing sixteen "colleges." He sits with the town's governor on a fortress wall encircling the monastery.

"One of the major revelations in going to Tibet is the thing that Harrer never seemed to write about in his book: a transformation by virtue of his contact with this incredible place," Johnston says. "When you go there, you think 'My God, you would have to be one of the living dead not to have this place affect your soul and everything about you.'"

What's more, in the course of her research, Johnston turned up a crucial fact about Harrer. When he set out to climb Nanga Parbat, he left behind his wife, who was pregnant, a fact never mentioned in *Seven Years*. By the time Johnston sat down to write the script, she found herself with an arc: an ambitious man leaves his wife and child to go climb a mountain; he fails but ends up in Tibet—where he undergoes a spiritual transformation, finds himself, and then returns home a different man.

This narrative allowed her to fold in other aspects of Harrer's story: his climbing exploits, his friendship with the Dalai Lama, his encounters with Buddhism. And as those levels began to meld, Johnston discovered the story could also be read as a fable of an achievement-driven Western man who is transformed by his contact with Eastern spirituality.

"To me, the whole thing was about a man who goes through a series of humiliations," Johnston said. "And eventually learns that the graceful way of accepting life is not to assert his ego."

The Karma of Casting

Like most veteran directors, Annaud has his own way of doing a film. For him, the script is key: as soon as he reads a script and it clicks emotionally, he is able to see the entire movie, shot by shot, in his head. From that point on, the challenge is to translate the pictures in his head to the screen and to recapture the emotions he experienced while reading the script. Everything—from the selection of lead actors to the color of smallest prop—is orchestrated around that goal. "For me, before I shoot a movie," Annaud says, "my movie is already playing in my head."

No sooner did Annaud read Johnston's script than it clicked, and he pulled out all the stops to get the movie that was already running in his head onto the screen. His enthusiasm was quickly shared. On a Friday, he discreetly sent out a few copies of the script from his Los Angeles office to top executives at TriStar; by Monday, his answering machine was loaded with calls from agents representing most of the leading talent in the country, inquiring about the role of Harrer.

"It was incredible, really," Annaud recalls. "Somehow virtually every major star had managed to get a hold of a copy, read it, and get back to me—in one weekend! I have no idea how that happened. . . . But that is how we met Brad."

The thirty-three-year-old actor was just coming off a series of performances—*Thelma & Louise, A River Runs Through It, Legends of The Fall, Interview with a Vampire*—that had established him as one of the top young box-office draws.

Born in Shawnee, Oklahoma, the son of a former trucking company manager and a high school guidance counselor, Pitt was raised in Springfield, Missouri. He set out to become a journalist at the University of Missouri, moved into advertising, then left college and made his way to Hollywood.

His breakthrough part came in *Thelma & Louise*, as a young cowboy hus-

tler with a charming grin and a pair of blue eyes. He was on-camera for only fifteen minutes but burned a hole through the screen. From there, Pitt's roles put him in the hearts and minds—and on the bedroom walls— of a lot of teenage girls, landed him on the cover of *Vanity Fair*, and boosted his salary per picture into the millions. At the same time, all the attention threatened to turn him into just another Hollywood Hunk.

Pitt had other ideas. He dealt with his media fame by immersing himself in his work and consciously looking for roles that expanded his range as an actor. He had two lined up: one as a police detective in an offbeat thriller called *Seven,* and another as a wacky environmentalist/terrorist in Terry Gilliam's strange science fiction film, *12 Monkeys.* Both roles would bring Pitt widespread critical acclaim—and an Oscar nomination for *12 Monkeys.*

Seven Years in Tibet fit right into Pitt's thinking. It was not a traditional Hollywood vehicle: indeed, for nearly half the movie, Harrer is portrayed as an incredibly selfish, arrogant, success-driven individual who will stop at nothing to "summit." But what sealed the deal in Pitt's mind was Annaud. They met for lunch in Los Angeles one day, spent most of the day talking, and quickly discovered a shared passion, on screen and off: photography.

"The first day I sat down with him, he had just got his pictures back from Tibet and northern India, the ones he took, and he was so excited to show them to me!" Pitt recalls. "I couldn't believe it, really. Here's a comfortable man. He's got money, a nice home, a family, whatever. He could be doing anything, you know—he could just be sitting in Paris, sipping cappucino all day. Instead, he's going to the depths of Vietnam, or trekking Madagascar, fighting insects, just to see the place! And he's sitting there telling me about his experiences traveling through the Himalayas, and he is so excited about it. How could you not get excited about it?"

That attitude was shared by the English actor David Thewlis, who was picked to play the key supporting role of Peter Aufschnaiter, the world-class climber who accompanied Harrer on his journey into Tibet.

Thewlis by age thirty had established himself as one of England's premier young actors. He was born and raised in the resort town of Blackpool in northern England, and studied at London's Guild Hall School of Music and Drama. He put together a body of British film and television work in the 1980s, including a part in Dennis Potter's legendary *The Singing Detective.*

But it was his work with the acclaimed director Mike Leigh that would bring Thewlis an international reputation. He had a small role in Leigh's *Life Is Sweet,* then took the lead as the blistering, self-destructive Johnny in *Naked,* which won him a Best Actor Award at Cannes in 1993.

He, too, clicked with Annaud on first meeting. "Quite honestly, I was worried when I first met him that he seemed too nice. He was so amiable and generous and passionate and sympathetic in our meetings, I immediately thought, 'Yeah, but I bet he's a bastard on the set. He can't really be this nice,'" Thewlis says. "But he really is—which is why I am so into him. . . . He's one of the very best directors I have ever worked with, and one of the nicest human beings I have ever had a relationship with."

Once the main characters were set, Annaud began to fill out his story with a predominantly Asian cast, since more than half of the film took place in Tibet among Tibetans. For the speaking roles, he selected a range of actors from around the globe. B. D. Wong, the American-born Chinese actor who won a Tony for his Broadway role in *M. Butterfly,* was picked for the devious Tibetan minister Ngawang Jigme. Mako, the well-known Japanese actor who picked up an Oscar nomination for his role in *The Sand Pebbles* with Steve McQueen, was chosen for the role of Kungo Tsarong, the Tibetan minister who befriends Harrer and Aufschnaiter when they first arrive in Lhasa. And Danny Denzongpa, one of India's biggest film stars—

he is literally mobbed anywhere he goes in his country—was chosen to play a pivotal member of the Tibetan cabinet, the Regent.

To fill out the rest of the cast, Annaud set his casting director, Priscilla John, to work scouring Tibetan Buddhist communities around the world.

She visited Tibetan schools, remote Indian villages, and virtually anywhere Tibetans had relocated. While John focused on Asia and Europe,

English actor David Thewlis took the key role of Harrer's climbing partner and friend Peter Aufschnaiter.

Jamyang Wangchuk plays the Dalai Lama at about age fourteen, shown here on the roof of the "Potala" set with the Regent, played by Danny Denzongpa.

Los Angeles-based casting director Francine Maisler covered the United States and Canada, looking for Tibetans and Asian actors.

Some finds were relatively easy. Seventy-five monks were selected from some half dozen Tibetan Buddhist monasteries in India. Others were found by hard work and serendipity—like Lhakpa Tsamchoe, the striking young woman who plays Pema Dorjee, the Lhasa tailor who marries Aufschnaiter. Lhakpa holds a B.S. in chemistry, biology, and zoology, and works for the Tibetan Youth Congress. She went dancing one night at a disco in Bangalore, India, and was discovered by casting director John.

A few were found by the kind of chance that only seem to happen in the movies. Annaud's Hong Kong-based casting director, Patricia Pao, had had no luck finding boys to play the young Dalai Lama at different ages. Then one night she answered the door of her Hong Kong apartment, and there stood a small, beautiful fourteen-year-old boy, asking if he might borrow a video.

The boy, Jamyang Wangchuk, son of a diplomat from the mountain kingdom of Bhutan, was visiting Pao's next door neighbor. Incredibly, Jamyang had an eight-year old brother, Sonam. Both eventually were cast as the young Dalai Lama.

But no matter where or how the "Tibetans" were found, they all seemed to share one thing: *Seven Years* was more than just a movie to them. That feeling was perhaps best symbolized by Jetsun Pema, sister of His Holiness, who, in a fascinating twist of casting, plays their mother in the film. Since the 1960s, Pema has been supervising the education of Tibetan children in exile. Based in Dharamsala, she now oversees some 10,000 students.

Jetsun Pema, the Dalai Lama's sister, in the role of the Great Mother.

Pema had never acted and was reluctant to do so, especially since she would be portraying her own mother. But she came around to the idea after talking it over with her brother, the Dalai Lama, who encouraged her to try. "You see, whatever we Tibetans are doing, we are doing for a purpose," Pema explains. "The hope of every Tibetan is to go back to Tibet one day—we all hope to go back and free Tibet some day. That is always very clear in the minds of Tibetans.

"So whether you are looking after Tibetan children," she continues, "or acting in a movie that is going to give more awareness about Tibet to the general public, it is the same thing."

Above, Dorjee Tsering as the very young Dalai Lama on his pillow throne, and opposite, Jamyang Wangchuk in the same role, different age.

The Deity in the Details

Over the years, Annaud has earned a reputation for his attention to details. In *Quest for Fire*, for example, he and screenwriter Gérard Brach invented four primitive tribes, each with its own culture, from body language to implements. To flesh out each tribe further, Annaud brought in the renowned linguist and novelist Anthony Burgess and noted anthropologist Desmond Morris.

"I don't want my movies to be just 'a movie,'" Annaud has said on more than one occasion. "Movies are becoming the most important vehicle of culture, of knowledge."

To achieve the kind of authenticity he wants, Annaud loves to master a subject. His learning is not that of an amateur enthusiast or hobbyist: he was trained as a scholar at the Sorbonne in Paris, and that rigor has carried over into his filmmaking. He thinks nothing of spending three to five years on a film, if that's what it takes to get it right.

What's more, Annaud has a strong sense of what the French call *exigence*—a drive to carry out a task thoroughly and completely. (It borders on the demonic.) For *The Name of the Rose*, Annaud spent months searching Europe for the right monastery at which to film his medieval mystery. When he couldn't find what he wanted, he built his own, outside Rome; it became the largest set in Europe since the making of *Cleopatra*.

Annaud brought the same kind of intensity to researching *Seven Years*. He spent 1994 and 1995 traveling around Tibet and Tibetan settlements in Bhutan, Nepal, and India with members of his production department and his wife, constant companion, second set of eyes, and all-around muse, Laurence.

Among other things, Annaud is a serious photographer who works with a Leica M-6, prefers a wide-angle lens—21 mm—and is not afraid to push the shutter. He took some 17,000 photographs of everything from the Potala in Lhasa to family portraits of yak herders in the remote Tibetan plains. These were not tourist shots, either; Annaud photographed with the attention of a professional anthropologist to record the look, feel, and smell of Tibetan culture. Along the way, he explored the way he wanted his movie to look. His pictures also caught the camera angles he wanted in his movie.

These photographs were charted by Laurence, developed, and compiled into booklike tomes, which were passed out to the production and costume departments as sort of a visual Bible and emotional grammar. (A small sampling is reproduced in this book, starting on page 63.)

"You know, when you dig into a country like this, it is not so much about landscapes and architecture," Annaud reflects. "It is first of all about people. I look at their costumes, I look at their shoes, I look at the way they braid their hair. It's not only getting to understand the behavioral aspects of a people but the mind of a people—their soul.

"What I wanted most of all was to see the country and feel the spirit myself—with the lamas and the monks, smell this very unique olfactory experience of rancid yak butter and the soot of butter lamps, mixed with the smell of incense," Annaud said. "It becomes a very specific, wonderful, nostril experience!"

* * *

While Annaud was busy assembling a sensory record of Tibet, his associate producer, Alisa Tager, was pulling together a small library on the country, its people, and its culture. The results of Tager's research were compiled into a three-inch-thick notebook, an extensive still picture file, and a collection of videos that captured just about every foot of film ever shot on Tibet.

"We put together a small video library," Tager says. "We had about

From sets to costumes to the replication of ritual, Seven Years in Tibet *is as faithful as possible to the Tibet of the 1940s.*

twenty-five videocassettes—the small kind that you can view on a Watchman—of specific themes like 'yak herding' or 'palaquin processions' or 'the Potala ceremonies.' The tapes were then cross-referenced to the script and put in a computer program.

"We had a printout of scene numbers, and next to each scene was a list of tapes that could serve as a visual reference," she adds. "So, for example, before filming the ice skating scene, Jean-Jacques could look at the video guide, check the scene number, and see that tapes 5, 12, and 20 might be applicable—they even contained footage from the 1950s in Tibet—and look at them before setting up the scene."

When Tager, who holds a B.A. in history from the University of California at Berkeley and an M.A. in international studies from Yale, couldn't find answers in her "library," she them got firsthand, in faxes from Tenzin Tethong, who had been hired by Annaud as an adviser on all things Tibetan. Born and raised in Lhasa, Tethong spent some fifteen years as a monk and served as prime minister for the Tibetan government-in-exile for a time, before moving to the United States.

Ask a question, any question, and the chances were that the answer was on file. What shape were the kites in Lhasa? (Square.) What shade of green were the military uniforms of the invading Chinese army? (Olive/khaki.) Was the father of His Holiness given a traditional Tibetan "sky burial"— a ceremony where the body is left out in the mountains for buzzards to pick clean—or cremated? (He was cremated.)

These details are anything but pedantic, as Annaud thrives on such knowledge. His goal is to re-create an emotional reality on screen. The more he knows about a particular culture, the better equipped he is to make his movie. And by the time Annaud steps onto the set on the first day of filming, he is an expert on the film's content.

That knowledge, combined with his vast technical expertise about all aspects of filmmaking, commands an enormous respect from everyone who deals with him. He can tell at a glance when the ceiling of a Tibetan house on the set is too high, the color of a monk's robe is the wrong shade of red, or the film being used isn't fast enough to catch the details in the shadows.

"There's a reason why this man takes several years before he does another film—it's an experience for him," Pitt says. "You look back, and every one of his films took years to make, years to get the script right, years to cast, years to design! Ask him about *The Bear*, and he'll tell you how he painted fields to get them to look right!...

"And we don't even have to talk about his eye," Pitt continues. "When he tells you something is not right, you don't question it at all.... The man *knows*."

Chasing Light, Dressing Souls

While Annaud's deep research continued, cinematographer Robert Fraisse was on a mission of his own: he was chasing light—in Tibet.

"Jean-Jacques thought I should go to Tibet and see the light for myself," Fraisse recalls. "He thought it was very important that I see the Potala, as well as all those temples there—to see just what the light was like inside with those very strange, small windows close to the floor, and the light from all the butter lamps."

Fraisse is no stranger to Annaud's way of filmmaking, having shot *The Lover* (which earned him an Oscar nomination) and *Wings of Courage.* He studied hundreds of Annaud's photographs of Tibet, then spent five days touring the country, visiting Lhasa, Shigatse, and Gyantse with just a guide, and came back with an eyeful. Never in his thirty-odd years as a cinematographer had he seen such dramatic contrasts between light and shade as he did in the "Land of Snows." Equally striking was the contrast between the dazzling outside light and the smoke-filled interiors of the temples. Even the sky was an unusual dark blue.

The trip provided grist for Fraisse, who set out to re-create the light of Tibet on location in Argentina.

"When I started shooting in Argentina, I realized the light was very similar to Tibet," Fraisse notes. "And the landscapes are similar, too. So when you start building sets which are really replicas of what you have seen

in Tibet, add seventy-five real monks coming from Dharamsala, seventy-five other Tibetans from all over the world, and authentic costumes, it all comes together.

"You are in Argentina but actually you have the Tibetan point of view," Fraisse adds. "So what you photograph is Tibet."

In Italy, costume designer Enrico Sabbatini was climbing mountains of his own to capture the look, feel, and texture of Tibet in thousands of costumes, which would clothe everyone from yak herders in the remote Changtang to the young Dalai Lama, regally attired for his coronation in Lhasa.

To that end, Sabbatini pulled together a virtual tailor's shop: two head tailors—one for men, one for women; five assistant tailors from Italy; fif-

Heinrich Harrer photo of a group of Khampa tribesmen. Among the toughest fighters in Tibet, they volunteered to be the Dalai Lama's rearguard during his flight. Here they wear fox fur hats and carry forked sticks to support their guns.

teen assistant tailors from Argentina; a dyer; and four to five people just to "age" fabrics with a Tibetan touch. The complete staff came to forty people, but even so they were hard pressed to turn out the 3,000 costumes required. The amount of silk needed alone was astonishing: some twenty-four meters per cast member.

Equally amazing was the variety of Tibetan garb. The array of hats alone was enough to tax the imagination. A full-fledged minister, for example, wore a *changa*, a brocade cap with a tassel, for ceremonial occasions; a round fur cap called a *pensha* while working in his office; and a simple felt hat for informal occasions. The intricate Tibetan dress code added to the complexity. The servants and attendants of nobles, for example, could wear a wide-brimmed hat known as a *sog-sha*, with red tassels all around the brim. But they could not wear the same hat ringed with fur: that was reserved for cabinet ministers.

Of course, when all was said and done, the costumes were not about fine fabrics or elegant designs, Sabbatini said. His job was to create historically accurate costumes that reflected, when possible, the emotional state of a given character. Harrer, for instance, arrives in Tibet after his arduous trek wearing tattered European clothes, a symbol of his emotional state. By the end of his stay, he is wearing Tibetan-style dress: a simple, striking maroon robe that symbolizes his spiritual transformation to a Buddhist point of view.

"A costume designer is not dressing a body but a character, a way to be, a mentality," Sabbatini declares. "It's a lot of psychological work. . . . We dress the inside of a character, not the outside. That's what makes us different from fashion designers: fashion is body dressing. Costume design is soul-dressing."

Actors into Athletes

The actors had homework to do as well. For Pitt and Thewlis, this meant learning to ice skate and to climb. It wasn't as easy as it might sound. For one thing, Pitt's superstardom had virtually destroyed any chance of him just showing up at a local skating rink, putting on some blades, and taking a few spins. So he and Thewlis began their initial skating lessons around midnight, in a rink rented just for them outside Los Angeles.

Learning to mountain climb was a bit touchier, and carried out on the sly. The idea of a $10 million star rappelling up and down cliffs was not something that was going to light up the faces of studio execs, their insurance carriers, or, for that matter, Brad's mother. (Mrs. Pitt was not informed until after the event, Pitt says.) So Annaud sent Pitt and Thewlis off to climb in Europe, under the watchful eye of associate producer Tager and two veteran Austrian mountaineers, Tom Raudaschl and Wolfgang Tonninger. (Both wound up playing small parts in the film.)

The group spent two weeks climbing, first in the Austrian Alps, then in the Italian Dolomites. And it wasn't just "hikes": Pitt and Thewlis practiced snow and ice manuevers, rock climbing, and even some glacier ascents. They also immersed themselves in the mountain climber's mentality, camping out during climbs and living off knapsack dinners.

For Thewlis, who underwent a rigorous physical training program during that summer to put some twenty pounds on his lanky, six-foot-four frame, the experience provided invaluable insight into his character. "It was a very, very useful, apart from actually just learning to climb," Thewlis remarks. "We were taught by two Austrian climbers, and that was great because we were playing two Austrian climbers [in the movie], so it was a chance to study the culture, the action, and general Austrian personality, simply by being there."

The Gathering Storm

By September 1996, cast and crew were arriving in Argentina from all over the world. They landed first in Buenos Aires, then took a two-hour flight to Mendoza, where the production was based, then traveled by car, bus, and truck an hour and a half up to Uspallata, in the heart of the Andes, where the first scenes were to be shot.

Several hundred cast members and costumes for seven or eight weeks of shooting had to be trucked up and housed. So did hundreds of production people and all of their gear: everything from hammers to cameras. (There were 525 people in the construction crew alone!) Then came the caterers, who had to provide food and drink for a minimum of three meals a day, plus a morning and afternoon break, for everybody working. Not

Heinrich Harrer photo of ice skating, an activity introduced by Harrer and which the Tibetans called "walking on knives." The group pictured here on the Kyichu River in Lhasa includes Lobsang Samten, the Dalai Lama's brother, in the center.

surprisingly, some 241 trucks, vans, buses, and cars were required for the move.

The flood of men, women, machines, costumes, and props soon swamped the little mountain town, which was just a handful of buildings at the intersection of two roads. It quickly soaked up all the available hotels and spilled over to a nearby Argentine army base, where Buddhist monks were housed in barracks.

But the real excitement didn't start until Pitt and Thewlis landed in

Director Annaud and his camera operator, Martin Kenzie, set up a tracking shot on location in the Argentine Andes.

Buenos Aires in mid-September, and found themselves chased across the airport tarmac by hordes of young girls and paparazzi. "Brad-o-mania," as one local paper called it, had begun and would last for the entire shoot in Argentina. The fan madness quickly rendered Pitt a prisoner of his trailer on the set, his sprawling house outside Mendoza ringed with a high brick wall, and two huge bodyguards, who chauffeured him around in a four-wheel-drive vehicle with tinted glass. They never left his side except when he went before the cameras.

"It was very interesting to see what Brad's life was like here," says David Thewlis. "He couldn't go out. He couldn't even leave his house! I could go to a bar in Mendoza, hang out, have a beer, whatever. He couldn't even do that without causing a riot." But, Thewlis adds, "His response was great—

he kept a very level head about it. His way of handling it was to remain totally focused on his work."

The Storms Break

Photography officially kicked off on September 30, 1996, in Uspallata, under unusual circumstances. There, in the midst of an enormous re-creation of the ancient city of Lhasa, the entire cast and crew took part in a special Buddhist blessing ceremony.

At first glance the scene looked like something out of the film itself: rows of Buddhist monks, attired in traditional gold and maroon robes, sat cross-legged in front of a makeshift altar on which rested a picture of His Holiness the Dalai Lama and a gold-colored statue of Buddha. As part of the ceremony, the monks presented Annaud with a special white scarf called a *khata* that had been blessed by the Dalai Lama himself. And for the rest of the day, the director—well-known for his clothes sense on the set and off—made the most of his gift: he walked around looking like some World War I aviator with the scarf around his neck, flapping in the wind.

The serenity was quickly disrupted as filming began in the foothills, and the production was hit continually by dust storms—called "twisters" by the locals—that covered the cast and crew in dirt, blinded the eyes, and knocked over lights. By the end of the first week, virtually everyone was suffering from a dust-induced cough and windburn.

So bad were the storms that Laurence Annaud was forced—under doctor's orders—to miss a few days of shooting with a nagging throat dis-order and a serious middle-ear infection. Her absence from the set was an unheard-of event in the annals of Annaud filmmaking.

Laurence is officially the script supervisor; she is responsible for chart-ing each and every take. Unofficially, she is the second set of eyes, ears,

Annaud and his wife and script supervisor, Laurence (left), view video replays on location, along with Brad Pitt and David Thewlis (right), in tattered travel costumes.

and brains for Jean-Jacques. She is, you could say, the director behind The Director. They have worked together on every film since *Quest For Fire*— except for *The Bear*, when Laurence was pregnant with their daughter, Louise. The relationship has deepened to the point where they seem to know, without so much as a word between them, what each scene requires and how to get it. Indeed, to watch Laurence on the set is to realize she has the makings of an A-list director, if she chose to go that route. In fact, she did direct commercials for a while before she met and married Jean-Jacques in 1982.

Fortunately, the weather did not deter Annaud, a veteran of difficult shoots. The worse the weather got, the more enthusiastic he became. Nature, after all, was providing another touch of reality to his story.

"What I've known in this business is a complacency among people, especially as you go down the road and become more successful—but not Jean-Jacques," observes Brad Pitt. "Here's a guy who still gets thrilled and excited every day. The worse the weather gets, the happier he is, you know. The harder the elements, the more he loves it. Wind, rain, dust in the eyes—people can't see, people are getting blown over, lights are getting blown over. He's thrilled. 'Yes, yes! I want to go now, this is natural. We must go *now*.' It's hysterical to watch."

Creating the "Real" Tibet

One thing Annaud quickly discovered was that his Tibetan monks made splendid actors. Years of Buddhist training in meditation had taught them to focus their energies totally in the moment—whether that moment was sitting in the lotus position, contemplating a mantra, or doing a stunt in a movie.

"They are absolutely fantastic. It's quite incredible—the idea of giving yourself as you are," Annaud says. "I had two incredible guys [monks] who had to play the Burly Guides. They were amazing actors—plus stuntmen! I'm not kidding you. When you ask a stuntman to make a fall, he makes a fall, but because he's a stuntman he falls like he thinks a good stuntman should fall in a movie.

"Not these Tibetans—these Burly Guides," Annaud relates. "You tell these guys, 'You slip, and then you fall.' And, well, that's just what they do: they slip and they fall! Just like that, like in life. They instinctively understand what is fake, and this is very interesting to me. It is almost like a theme in this movie: 'being' instead of 'pretending.' And when the Tibetans are in front of the camera, they *are*."

Equally surprising for Annaud were the several hundred Bolivian extras, who bore an uncanny resemblance to Tibetan monks once they shaved their heads and dressed in maroon robes. Indeed, they were indistinguishable from their Tibetan counterparts—except they spoke Spanish.

"I have been using as many real Tibetans as I can," Annaud says. "That's the key of it—not to lose the Tibetan spirit. . . . But I can use Bolivians, they are remarkably similar. It's fine if I have 200 Bolivians in the background, as long as I put 150 Tibetans in the foreground."

Not just the performers, but their physical surroundings were incredibly true to Tibetan reality. On the sets outside Uspallata, the production department, under production designer At Hoang and art director Pierre Queffelean, brought to a life a 220-yard street in the heart of Lhasa. The buildings lining the street were replicas of their counterparts in Tibet: their walls slanted slightly in, Tibetan style; their post-and-lintel construction was brightly colored in blues and oranges; and the walls were cracked and chipped to look ancient. The cobblestone pavement was littered with real yak hair and yak dung for a pungent, authentic touch. Seeing all this against the backdrop of the Andes, it was hard to believe you were not in Tibet.

But the Lhasa sets were nothing compared with what was going up back at the ranch in San Martin, a little town just outside Mendoza, where crews worked around the clock to bring to life an astonishing world. The production took over a series of abandoned garlic warehouses and transformed them into a sprawling Hollywood back lot, which formed the hub of a series of satellite sets on the lot and off.

There were many. The Potala, it seemed, was being re-created room by room. In one warehouse, the *kashag*—meeting room of the ministers—was going up; it covered 4,500 square feet and came complete with long benches for the ministers and a throne for His Holiness. Next door, in another warehouse, the "Hall of Good Deeds"—the coronation room of the Dalai Lamas—was rising. This covered some 9,000 square feet, stretched a full three stories tall, and boasted usable balconies and stairs for all three floors.

Meanwhile, outside, the dramatic steps of the Potala ascended like some strange Mayan pyramid, four and half stories high. They totaled seventy-four steps, each about ten feet long and a foot wide.

Some ninety miles away, another world was under construction: the British prisoner-of-war camp at Dehra Dun, where Harrer and Aufschnaiter were held prisoner and escaped. This comprised twenty-six separate buildings covering 49,212 square feet, ringed with rolls of barbed wire.

The size and scope of the sets were outdone only by their riveting detail. The walls of the *kashag*, for example, were decorated with glass-enclosed floor-to-ceiling cabinets, each filled with shelves of small golden Buddhas or elaborate prayer rolls. They glowed mysteriously in the light of dozens of small bronze butter lamps—the Tibetan equivalent of votive candles—that ringed the room.

The production of Buddhas was a minor cottage industry at the Mendoza studio. One shed on the lot was devoted to their creation; they were molded from aluminum, filled with sand to give them weight, then painted gold. Hundreds were made that way, in all sizes from six inches to three feet tall. Traditional Tibetan items that could not be re-created by hand were copied, often inventively. The walls of the "Hall of Good Deeds," for example, were covered with paintings of Buddhas from floor to the ceiling. Their detail and coloring was astonishing: each one looked hand-painted and beautifully aged. And they were—in a way.

"Thank God for copier machines," says executive producer Richard Goodwin, who numbers among his credits David Lean's *A Passage To India*.

The movie set of the British prisoner-of-war camp in northern India from which Harrer and his compatriots escaped.

"We would never have been able to afford this without them.... What we did was to make photocopies of this particular Buddha, then paste the copies onto the wall like wallpaper and hand-color them."

"The incredible thing is," Goodwin adds with a smile, "they look absolutely real!"

Crowning Moments

All this attention to detail was not without purpose. That became evident shortly after Annaud, cast, and crew finished up shooting at Uspallata in early December and returned to Mendoza to shoot the coronation scene of the young Dalai Lama inside the "Hall of Good Deeds."

The enormous room was finally finished—all 9,000 square feet of it—and looked like some surreal dream of ancient Tibet come alive. The set was filled with row upon row of monks in maroon and gold robes; Tibetan noblemen arrayed in silk brocade of orange, blue, and red; and cabinet ministers, elegantly attired in long robes and large-brimmed hats trimmed with fur. All faced a throne made of golden silk pillows piled four feet high, where the Dalai Lama (played by fourteen-year-old Jamyang Wangchuk) sat, awaiting his crown.

Adding to the aura were long, streaming prayer banners that dangled from the upper balconies like giant, colorful kite tails. Banks of Tibetan butter lamps encircled the room, casting a haunting golden glow that illuminated countless Buddhas staring out wide-eyed from the wall, with one hand raised in the mudra of "no fear."

Lording over the room was a towering golden statue of Sakyamuni, the historical Buddha, who sat cross-legged on his lotus throne, decorated with fourteen intricate butter sculptures handmade by monks from a mixture of yak butter, wax, and water, in shades of pale pink, faint blue, and cream.

Annaud, dressed all in white, was hard to miss in this sea of brilliant colors. He darted around the set radiating enthusiasm, whether he was adjusting the horn-rimmed glasses of the young Dalai Lama or discussing a camera placement with his cinematographer, Fraisse. The director took particular joy in attending to small details—like the timing between the Tibetan ceremonial band (complete with long-horns) off to one side of the throne, and the chanting of the monks in the first row.

"First the music starts, then after a few bars we want the monks to start chanting," he said, pointing to the first row of monks. "And *then* they can start bowing."

It was eerie, in fact, how all the seemingly disparate elements came

together when Annaud shouted "Action!," and cameras rolled. The band struck up, the chanting began, and as row after row of monks began bowing, a wave of human flesh seemed to recede from the throne, back through the hall, finally focusing attention on the only white face in the crowd: Harrer (Pitt). He sat near the last row, dressed in a simple but stunning wine-colored robe, and he was bowing, just like everyone else.

That, of course, was the point. The entire scene—the building, people, costumes, lighting, music—had been orchestrated to dramatize an emotional point: The world-class mountain climber has exchanged his awards and climbing spikes for a sense of compassion and a simple red robe. He is now part of Buddhist culture.

As that awareness dawned, the smell of incense suddenly became very evident. It was everywhere, hanging in clouds and emanating from behind the Dalai Lama's throne of pillows. And as one traced the source of the cloud, there was Annaud, hidden behind the throne, happily waving sticks of Tibetan incense.

"I wanted to smell it," he explains. "And I wanted my Tibetan friends to smell it, too. It is the perfume of their country and when they smell it, they are there!"

The emotions generated in these scenes often lingered long after the cameras stopped rolling, particularly for the Tibetans. Indeed, at times it was hard to know where the movie stopped and life began.

In one scene, for example, a crowd of Tibetans was forced to watch their leaders surrender to the Chinese. The emotional core of the scene was a cry by the young Lhasa tailor, Pema, "Give the Dalai Lama the power to free Tibet!" But no sooner were the cameras rolling, and the treaty signed, and the cry "Free Tibet!" went up, than the chant was picked up by others and began to echo around the set. The chant continued long after Annaud yelled "Cut!"—and left a good many of cast and crew in tears.

"Many of the older monks who are in this movie are actually reliving things that have happened to them," said Jetsun Pema. "There are scenes in this movie, you know, where the invading Chinese troops are forcing young monks to shoot their own teachers. That actually happened in Tibet."

"For the younger Tibetans involved in this film—those twenty to twenty-five, or thirty, who were born in India and have never seen Tibet— they are learning so much about their past," she continues. "It has brought together Tibetans from all over the world—from India, Europe, America. And that would have not happened had it not been for this movie."

The learning experience, it seems, was not one-sided. In Mendoza, for example, many of the monks housed at a downtown hotel suddenly found themselves celebrities as they walked around town in their traditional gold and maroon robes, wearing matching maroon Converse low-cuts and, in some cases, wraparound sunglasses. They were stopped on the street and photographed, and cheered in the local shopping malls when they showed up.

On another level, the palpable spirituality of the monks deeply affected many of the Western cast and crew, who came to see them as remarkable individuals. They had lost friends, family, their homes, their country—and yet retained a profound serenity and a deep kindness that affected anyone who came near them.

"There have been a lot of times during this film when we've had experiences that we would not have had had we gone to Tibet as tourists," Thewlis said. "This is not just a rare opportunity to understand another culture. It is a *unique* opportunity. . . . We are living with them on a daily basis and have got to know several of them very well."

"I even had a great jam session with them at this wonderful party they threw for us," recalls Thewlis. "I sat down and started playing their four-string guitar, sang for about an hour, and in the middle of that I was thinking, 'Wow, this is a pretty unique occasion.' I have never sat in the middle of a hundred Tibetan monks playing guitar and feeling so loved! . . . You'd never get this in a London pub."

To the Heights

Principal photography in Argentina wrapped on January 23, 1997, in La Plata, a small town outside Buenos Aires. Here were shot the opening sequences of the film, where Harrer bids his pregnant wife goodbye in Austria and takes off to climb Nanga Parbat.

Two weeks later, a modified cast and crew—about a hundred, all told—were in Canada, ensconced in a base camp of Winnebagos and ATCO trailers on a small ranch near Mount Waddington (a two-and-a-half hour plane

Continued on page 67

A PORTFOLIO OF IMAGES

by Jean-Jacques Annaud

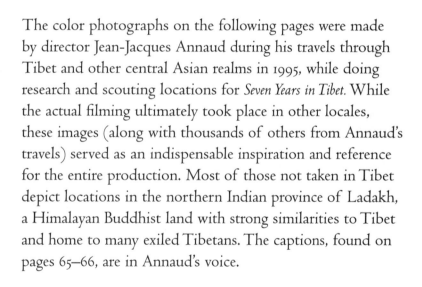

The color photographs on the following pages were made by director Jean-Jacques Annaud during his travels through Tibet and other central Asian realms in 1995, while doing research and scouting locations for *Seven Years in Tibet*. While the actual filming ultimately took place in other locales, these images (along with thousands of others from Annaud's travels) served as an indispensable inspiration and reference for the entire production. Most of those not taken in Tibet depict locations in the northern Indian province of Ladakh, a Himalayan Buddhist land with strong similarities to Tibet and home to many exiled Tibetans. The captions, found on pages 65–66, are in Annaud's voice.

CAPTIONS FOR COLOR PHOTOGRAPHS
BY JEAN-JACQUES ANNAUD

1. Gyatse, the third largest city in Tibet. The fortress that once guarded the town—or what remains of it—is seen from the top of the sacred Palkhor Chode, one of the most revered Tibetan sanctuaries.

2. The Yamzho Yung Lake, near the 15,000-foot pass on the high road between Lhasa and Gyantse, in Tibet.

3. Travelers on a dirt road in the hills near Leh, the capital of Ladakh, in far northern India.

4. A Tibetan woman in the Barkhor, Lhasa.

5. Pilgrims in a small street of the Barkhor, the old bazaar of Lhasa. At right are the prayer wheels of Tibetan Buddhism, set spinning to carry prayers to the gods. This small street, along with the whole district, was destroyed a few months after I took this picture.

6. The Potala Palace, formerly the Dalai Lama's residence in Lhasa, seen from the roof of the Jokhang temple.

7. A brilliantly painted corridor in the Potala. The world's largest palace, it has about a thousand rooms.

8. Behind the Potala, pilgrims circumnambulate along the lower walk of the sacred fortress. The walk, always followed counterclockwise, is several miles long, and there are several hundred prayer wheels to be spun along the way.

9. Sacred goldfish in the small lake behind the Potala.

10. The rooftops of the Jokhang in Lhasa, Tibet's most sacred temple.

11. Gold-leafed *gyaltsen*, or "banners of victory," surmount the roof of the Jokhang.

12. An ornate door at the Jokhang temple. The colored cloth hanging from the rings is brown from the yak butter on the hands of countless pilgrims.

13. Lamayuru, one of the most famous villages in Ladakh. The red building, as always, is the monastery.

14. Below the Payang Monastery in Ladakh, *chortens,* or monuments to distinguished Buddhists, stand in alignment.

15. Two monks blowing ornamented conches on the roof of Tikse Monastery, Ladakh.

16. On the steps of Tikse Monastery.

17. An arcaded and painted wall at Tikse Monastery.

18. Prayer wheels and *chorten*s at Lamayuru, Ladakh.

19. A monk in his cell at the Lamayuru Monastery beats on a drum while reading Buddhist scriptures.

20. The main prayer chamber at Tikse Monastery.

21. Young monks refilling yak butter lamps at Lamayuru Monastery.

22. Monks on a terrace overlooking the fields outside Lamayuru, Ladakh, during monsoon season.

23. On the roof of the Jokhang in Lhasa, after a hailstorm.

ride from Vancouver) and ready to film the mountaineering sequences.

Annaud knew the terrain well—he had scouted the area for his IMAX 3-D venture, *Wings of Courage*. Its remote, desolate beauty (the nearest town, Williams Lake, is four hours away by car) was just what the director needed for *Seven Years*—even if some days it took a forty-five-minute helicopter ride just to reach the "set" where the day's shooting took place.

"It is the only other place on earth—outside the Himalayas—where there is this huge differential between summits and valleys, with gigantic glaciers everywhere," Annaud explains. "The average elevation of the coastal range is about six thousand feet lower than the Himalayas, but it has almost the identical look. And the lower altitude is much better for actors, filmmakers . . . and helicopters."

The scenery was breathtaking—indeed, more than one cast member remarked that this was the most beautiful place on earth they had ever seen. But this heaven had its downside, particularly after the novelty wore off during the first two weeks, and the reality of either spending the day cooped up in a six-by-ten-foot room, reading or watching videos (there was one VCR in camp), or outside, dressed to the nines, slogging through knee-deep snow, trying to cope with the prevailing subzero temperatures and blistering Artic winds sank in.

Contributing to the stress was an interesting dilemma: the production needed bad weather for the climbing scenes it was filming, but if the weather was too bad, the helicopters couldn't fly the cast and crew to the set. That meant long hours waiting for the right mix of conditions.

The boredom, however, was mixed with real terror. The climbing scenes being filmed were risky, and strong winds kept the adrenaline flowing. One shot, in particular, was nerve-racking: Harrer and Aufschnaiter are climbing up a steep slope when Aufschnaiter slips, slides down the icy slope, and falls off a cliff—only to be caught by his rope, which is tied to

Harrer. He is left dangling in midair. To capture the shot, the camera crew set up a platform at the top of the slope, tied themselves in, and hoped for the best as the wind blew.

"All the shots were shot in an outstanding landscape but it was a very scary place," says cinematographer Fraisse. "It was really dangerous because there was a real cliff, and the platform was very small and very slippery with ice. The security people were very nervous, and we were all roped in.

"Brad and David were very courageous," Fraisse added. "They had been trained in the Dolomites for two weeks before the movie started. We didn't use any stuntmen in this particular scene. When Aufschnaiter 'falls' twenty meters [about seventy feet] he really falls—and is really caught by his rope."

The Art and *Exigence* of Post-production

The filming in Canada wrapped on March 8, 1997, and within forty-eight hours Annaud had put Laurence on a plane to Paris, taken his own plane to London, and was set up in his editing room, piecing together his film.

Actually, Annaud had been working on editing the film since the first days in Argentina. He would come home each night after putting in twelve- to fourteen-hour days on the set, eat dinner, then sit down at a Steinbeck viewing table in the back room and watch dailies. He would make notes on which shots he liked and why, and mail them off to his editor in London, Nöelle Boisson, another veteran of Annaud's filmmaking wars.

"She was my preferred editor when I was a commercial director," Annaud says, explaining his choice. "And she has cut *The Bear* and *The Lover*. We work very, very well together—and she is the most respected (and awarded) editor in France!"

As a rule, Annaud likes to start editing his films from the beginning. But in this case, the opening scenes—those with Harrer and Aufschnaiter climbing—were not yet printed when he sat down to work. So he began as best he could, fitting together a narrative.

"The first assembly is always so horrifying that you have take some steps to shape something," Annaud said. "You have to go in, explain the intent of each scene, try to give it a [dramatic] shape, and then 'see' a sequence like twenty minutes long. What I try to do, the first time around, is give a shape to scenes and sequences that at least is pleasurable to watch. And begin to juggle the continuity from there."

For the next eight weeks, Annaud and Boisson worked around the clock, putting in, on the average, fourteen-hour days, six days a week. Lunch was takeout, eaten on the corner of an editing table; dinner was a frozen entrée, microwaved and eaten out of the container at 11:30 P.M.

As the film began to take shape, Annaud discovered the biggest challenge was to provide a cohesive narrative, visually and dramatically, that knit together the various levels of the story—the personal, the Tibetan, and the historical. "What was very difficult in the editing was keeping those epic aspects, emotional aspects, historical aspects together," Annaud says. "To tell you the truth, it is very, very tough and I was very worried that the different layers would not jell. . . . It is very difficult to work with multiple layers. . . . But that's also the challenge of it, and the charm."

Part of the glue that holds the story together would be supplied by the legendary composer John Williams, who numbers among his credits such blockbusters as *Star Wars* and *Indiana Jones,* and was now looking to stretch his talents into another direction.

"John—very much like Brad—was tired of doing all the time what he is very much famous for, and was excited to try something different," Annaud notes, "to score the melody of a heart instead of enhancing the muscle of special effects.

"John is one of the very, very rare composers who is very familiar with

Heinrich Harrer's photo of the Dalai Lama at age sixteen, the last photograph taken of His Holiness in free Tibet. Surrounded by his ministers, he holds an golden urn containing the relics of Gautama Buddha, which he is blessing.

classical symphonic music *and* film," he adds. "He has incredible understanding of the 'needs' of assembled images."

On the visual level, Annaud was looking to create a framework that would pull the viewers into the film, then keep them hooked. To do that, he began to build his scenes in such a way as to create a visual question with a shot or two, answer his question in a following shot, then pose another question in the next shot, which would start the process all over again.

For instance, the film opens with a shot in the middle of a barren mountain landscape, then focuses in on Tibetan noblemen, splendidly dressed. What is going on? The camera moves in to tell us: we see the nobles are bringing presents. For whom? The camera moves again and shows us: the young Dalai Lama sitting on his throne. He is opening a present—it is a large music box.

"This movie was very much written like that: a scene raises questions, and you get the answer in the next scene," Annaud says. "I do that usually, but I did that more this time, where a shot would be incomplete. . . . I like that because it keeps the attention of the audience alive."

"I don't like telling you the story and closing the story," he elaborates. "If you close the story, you close the scene, and if you close the scene, you close the movie. I like to be constantly having the audience trying to figure something out—'Am I sure about this?' Because then there is participation, almost interactivity, instead of just being passive."

The director considers for a moment, then smiles and adds, "Definitely, I am trying to keep the audience alive with a few questions."

I.

4.

5.

8.

9.

II.

12.

15.

18.

19.

20.

21.

22.

23.

25.

26.

27.

The

SCREENPLAY

❧

by Becky Johnston

FADE IN:

Credit Sequence

EXT. TIBETAN VALLEY — DAY

The DEEP DRONE of CHANTING rises over a the image of a primordial, monumental landscape—a huge bowl of blue sky, a ridge of snow-capped mountains defining the edges of a vast plateau. In a fertile valley, a sprawling tent encampment comes into view. Enormous ceremonial tents are covered with Asian symbols.

INT. TENT — DAY

Inside the largest tent, hordes of exotically dressed ASIAN NOBLES in brocades and fur, MONKS in crimson robes, march in single file up an aisle, bearing gifts. All are CHANTING in a low, monotonous susurration. An elderly MONK carries a beautiful Oriental lacquer MUSIC BOX with the image of a mountain on its lid. The crowds of worshippers keep their eyes cast downward, continue CHANTING as they place their gifts in front of a tall throne emblazoned with snow lions.

ON THE THRONE: Sits a young Tibetan boy of four. He is the DALAI LAMA. He rests cross-legged and sustains a pose of preternatural calm while the gifts are displayed for his inspection. Beside the Dalai Lama—on two smaller thrones at lower levels—sit his PARENTS. Growing restless on his high, lonely perch, the boy leans down and whispers to his mother.

> DALAI LAMA
>
> Ama...Ama la...

Sitting erect and proud, the mother does not glance at her son, shakes a reproving finger. The boy visibly shrinks and retreats, longing for contact. Then, suddenly, his mobile face brightens with pleasure as the elderly monk holds out the MUSIC BOX, opens it, and a haunting lullaby springs from it. Beaming, the Dalai Lama extends his hand to touch the box.

End Credits

INT. CAR — DAY

HEINRICH HARRER—a cocky, flaxen athlete who looks like the poster boy for *Triumph of the Will*—stares out the window, trying to suppress his anger as his young wife, INGRID, vents her frustration. Once a beautiful woman, Ingrid is pale, sullen, emotionally fragile.

> INGRID
>
> I wish we'd said goodbye at the front door and it was finished. And you could have a nice and pleasant journey on your own.

Harrer turns to her, fed up.

HARRER

Why must you be this way? Why is there always a problem?
It's a good question. Life is not always convenient.
(*pretending to humor her*)
Do you want to go home, do you want to turn around?

INGRID

Yes.

HARRER

It's the Himalayas! How long have I been talking about the
Himalayas? How long?

Ingrid seems to retreat into herself, shaken.

INGRID

Far too long.

A meek man—HORST IMMENDORF—drives the car, pretending to ignore
the tensions in the back seat. Ingrid leans forward.

INGRID

Horst, when we get there, can you give me a hand?

HORST

Yes, of course.

Harrer rolls his eyes, thinks she's begging for sympathy.

HARRER

Oh, Ingrid. Stop it.

EXT. GRAZ TRAIN STATION — DAY

The car stops across from the busy station; NAZI SOLDIERS stream toward
the entrance, above which hangs a huge swastika flag. Harrer gathers his
rucksack, takes Ingrid's hand and leads her through the crowds.

HARRER

Try to make this pleasant.

INT. GRAZ TRAIN STATION TICKET ROOM — DAY

The station is teeming with more Nazi soldiers. Harrer drags Ingrid past TRAVELERS waiting in line to purchase tickets, searching for someone.

HARRER

Where is that idiot who's supposed to meet us?

Spotting Harrer, a tall thin MAN of exquisite precision approaches him: PETER AUFSCHNAITER. Aufschnaiter has a stack of tickets in his hand.

AUFSCHNAITER

Mister Harrer? I have your tickets—

Harrer grabs the tickets from Aufschnaiter's hands.

> HARRER
> Fine. I'm late. Take me to my train—

> AUFSCHNAITER
> No, no, no. You don't understand...
> *(modestly)*
> I am Peter Aufschnaiter. I'm leading the expedition.
> How do you do?

Smiling shyly, Aufschnaiter extends a hand. Sizing up this unprepossessing man, Harrer shakes Aufschnaiter's hand, wearing an expression of acute disappointment.

INT. TRAIN STATION AND PLATFORMS — DAY

As Harrer, Ingrid, and Horst emerge from the ticket room into the station, they see two platforms up ahead where the crowd of German SOLDIERS file onto trains. Departing one of the tracks, a line of flatbed cars stacked with artillery, tanks.

As Harrer, Ingrid, and Horst make their way toward their train, a robust NAZI OFFICIAL spots Harrer and makes a beeline toward him.

> OFFICIAL
> Ah, here's our celebrity.
> *(reaches Harrer)*
> May I say, Mr. Harrer, on behalf of the Reichssportsfuhrer,
> we are honored to have such a great German hero on the team.

> HARRER
> Thank you. But I'm Austrian.

Leading Harrer past throngs of people, the Official gestures to the Photographer who hurries over as the Official grandly presents Harrer with a small Nazi flag. The Photographer snaps a photo.

OFFICIAL

Yes, but I'm sure that, as a distinguished member of the National Socialist Party, you will be proud to plant our country's flag on the summit of Nanga Parbat...when you reach it.

(slowing down)

I am quite sure the man who conquered the Eiger North Wall can subdue the gods of "our mountain" in the Himalayas.

Harrer takes the flag. CAMERAS FLASH. They reach a car where Aufschnaiter is waiting with two other climbers: HANS LOBENHOFFER and LUTZ CHICKEN, a kind of German Frick and Frack duo. The two teammates extend their hands to offer introductions to Harrer.

LOBENHOFFER

Hans Lobenhoffer.

CHICKEN

Lutz Chicken.

Harrer dutifully shakes their hands. CAMERAS FLASH.

OFFICIAL

And a picture with your lovely wife.

Harrer shoots Ingrid an imploring look, pulls her close to him. She smiles wanly when the CAMERAS FLASH. The Official gestures to Horst.

OFFICIAL

And Mister...

HORST
Horst Immendorf. Family friend. No picture necessary.

As the Photographer fires off a few more shots, Harrer flashes a bright, exuberant smile—in sharp contrast to the impacted sorrow underlying Ingrid's smile. He has perfected a breezy public persona, and the effort-lessness of his act only adds to her misery.

OFFICIAL
(pointing)
When is the little one due, Mrs. Harrer?

He is pointing to Ingrid's belly. And for the first time, the CAMERA REVEALS what has been hidden: Ingrid is seven and a half months pregnant. The question strikes her deep in the heart. And causes Harrer's smile to fade.

INGRID

Approximately the same time as my husband reaches
base camp.

With that, she breaks away and visibly struggles to keep her emotions in
check. Harrer grabs her, drags her away from the media onslaught.

HARRER

Why don't you tell the whole country our problems?

Her eyes brim with tears; she is close to breaking down.

HARRER

I'm getting on that train. Is there anything you want to
say to me?

She stares mutely at him, appalled by his lack of feeling.

HARRER

Fine. Go. I'll see you in four months.

Trying to conceal his mounting sense of shame, he kisses her, then turns to
Horst, anxious to get away.

HARRER

Take good care of her.

INT. TRAIN — DAY

Pushing through a maze of bodies, Harrer stops by a window, peers out, sees:

EXT. PLATFORM — POV — THROUGH WINDOW:

Ingrid and Horst turning away from the platform, heading through the station. She is crying uncontrollably. Horst wraps his arm around her, tries to
console her.

INT. TRAIN — DAY

Harrer watching, consumed with guilt. He moves down the aisle, passing a compartment where the three other members of his team are already seated. An empty spot is waiting for Harrer.

Unable to face them, Harrer keeps moving, heads into another compartment.

INT. TRAIN COMPARTMENT — LATER

As the train hurtles through the Tirolean countryside, Harrer sinks into despair, staring blankly out the window.

POV — THROUGH WINDOW: Outside, a white curtain of clouds parts to reveal an isolated peak rising from the great chain of the Tauern Alps.

CLOSE UP — MAP OF WORLD

A map showing the course of Harrer's journey, through Europe by train, into Asia by boat. Toward a mountain peak in the Himalayas—the name, Nanga Parbat.

HARRER'S VOICE narrates as we follow the winding path toward his destination.

> HARRER (V.O.)
> We will travel five thousand miles. When we reach India, we will head for the Himalayas and the ninth highest peak on Earth, Nanga Parbat. The name means "Naked Mountain." Germany calls it Unser Berg, "Our Mountain." Before us, four German expeditions attempted it. All failed. Eleven climbers were killed in storms and avalanches. By now, the conquest of Nanga Parbat is a national obsession, a matter of German pride.

EXT. MOUNTAIN — DAWN

Lit by a luminous full moon, the four German climbers hike across a glacial ridge on Nanga Parbat.

EXT. NANGA PARBAT — DAY

Advancing up a steep ice slope, the team moves with careful precision, digging their axes into the ice.

Harrer's VOICE continues the narration.

> HARRER (V.O.)
> July 29, 1939. We have already made Camp Four at 22,000 feet. Overhead is the Rakhiot Glacier and a difficult climb up the icefall.
> *(pauses)*
> The baby must be at least one month old now. I have been so confused and distracted, I can't climb with my usual confidence.

At the rear, Harrer seems out of sync with the others, his mind elsewhere. He takes a step. His foot slips. He loses balance. Slides down the slope, legs twisting and flailing, jams his foot into his calf. The sharp metal points of his crampons impale his calf, ripping the flesh. In agonizing pain, he manages to arrest the fall with his ice axe. Far above him, out of eyesight, the others shout to Harrer.

> AUFSCHNAITER
> Are you all right?

> HARRER
> Yeah, lost a crampon. Go on ahead.

He glances down—the snow beneath him is soaked with blood. Shaking and pale, he examines his calf. Blood pours from the open wound. He quickly

wraps a tourniquet around it, furious with himself. Makes a point of hiding the tourniquet under his sock. Washes blood off his sock with snow.

EXT. NANGA PARBAT — DAY

Higher up, storm clouds have settled over a ridge. Lobenhoffer and Chicken are roped together, climbing as a team. Farther down, Harrer grimaces as he limps up the slope toward Aufschnaiter, quickly hides the fact that he's hurting when he reaches him.

> AUFSCHNAITER
> The weather's getting bad. We should rope up.

Harrer nods and the two of them uncoil their ropes, hook them to each other's harnesses.

> AUFSCHNAITER
> Did you hurt yourself back there?

> HARRER
> Just a scratch.
> *(finishes roping up)*
> I'll lead.

EXT. ROCK FACE — DAY

CLOSE ON HARRER'S LEG: Blood oozing from the sock. Harrer in the lead, fighting against blistering wind and snow. He climbs with single-minded intensity, unaware of the pain. Finds a hold and buoys himself up the ridge, glancing down at Aufschnaiter—thirty feet below him, scaling the wall.

AUFSCHNAITER has one foot in a step, pulls himself up to a small natural platform jutting from rock face.

Suddenly, from higher up, a ROCK SLIDE. Harrer shouts from the ridge as the rocks tumble toward Aufschnaiter.

> HARRER
> Rocks!

AUFSCHNAITER loses his footing—and abruptly plunges. Then stops, dangling off the edge of the face. The only thing keeping him from plummeting thousands of feet is the belay rope held by Harrer.

HARRER ON RIDGE grimaces as he assumes a squatting brake position, holds tight with both hands. His wounded leg starts to spasm and wobble, the exertion causes the blood to SPURT. Panicking, he peers down at

AUFSCHNAITER, dangling off the side of rock face. He claws at the rock with his axe, desperate for a hold.

HARRER ON LEDGE is losing strength from the profusion of blood. Trying vainly to stem the flow, he drops one hand from the rope and clamps it tightly over the wound. In one fell swoop, he loses his pivot and twenty feet of rope slip from his grasp.

AUFSCHNAITER tumbles farther down the precipice, terrified. At an acute angle from the wall, he uses all his strength to fashion a foot stirrup with his rope, enabling him to shimmy up the rope as

HARRER ON LEDGE keeps belaying, never loosening his grip, despite his deteriorated condition. When Aufschnaiter finally makes it to the ledge, he sinks to the ground. The two men are too shaken to speak for a moment.

Harrer coils up his rope, stiffens when Aufschnaiter takes a good look at his bloody, injured leg.

> AUFSCHNAITER
> You should have told me how bad that wound was.

Harrer keeps pretending to be busy coiling rope.

> AUFSCHNAITER
> You want me to look at it? I could stitch it up.

> HARRER
> It's not your problem.

Taken aback by Harrer's dismissive tone, Aufschnaiter becomes annoyed.

> AUFSCHNAITER
> Actually, it is my problem. It's my life.

> HARRER
> What?

> AUFSCHNAITER
> When someone conceals a serious wound from me and puts
> my life at risk, I consider that my problem.

Harrer snorts, full of righteous scorn.

                              HARRER
         No, you put your life at risk, I saved it, so shut up.

Disgusted by Harrer's attitude, Aufschnaiter's face hardens.

                          AUFSCHNAITER
         Next time you lie about an injury, Heinrich, you're off
         the team.

EXT. ROOF OF PALACE — DUSK

TWO MONKS in crimson blow long silver trumpets. A sonorous WAIL rever-
berates through the valley below. The slow THUDDING of a DRUM is heard.

EXT. PALACE — DUSK

Like a dream image, a mystical palace rises from a rocky hillside. The palace
is stained deep umber and white. It is multistoried, crisscrossed by long,
winding flights of steps. People on the street perform prostrations to its
towering presence.

EXT. PALACE ROOF — DUSK

More monks wearing huge keys tied to their waists ascend the steps to the
roof, locking doors on their way.

INT. DOORWAY TO MAIN COURTYARD — PALACE — DUSK

The DRUMBEAT continues, monks close doors on the last rays of sunlight.
In darkness, they clamp enormous locks over the latches and lock them
with the keys.

INT. PALACE — DUSK

Bodyguards in huge padded robes are stationed outside a suite of rooms.
Monks in crimson robes pass the rooms and bow in reverence.

INT. SUITE OF ROOMS — DUSK

MOVING LIKE A GHOST through an empty waiting room, the walls adorned with intricate murals; statues of wrathful deities glower in the waning twilight.

INT. BEDROOM — DUSK

Lying wide awake in his ornate, carved wood bed is the five-year-old DALAI LAMA. His bedroom is a kind of sprawling crypt; dark, musty, the ancient walls stained with smoke from hundreds of butter lamps illuminating the blackness. Hanging from the walls are dusty but resplendent tapestries—*thangkas*—meticulously detailed portraits of Buddhas, Bodhisattvas, Arhats, and Dakinis. Below the *thangkas,* a shrine on which rest exquisite statues of the five Buddhas. Gold bowls filled with water, lotus flowers, barley, incense—as offerings. More offerings of fruit and bread. Hordes of hungry mice devour the fruit and bread, flit across the room like nervous demons.

The Dalai Lama looks trapped in the huge bed, too frightened to sleep. He tiptoes over to a window, peers longingly at the world outside.

POV — THROUGH WINDOW — DUSK

In the distance, the Himalayas form a glowing, murky white barrier to the south.

EXT. CAMP FIVE, NANGA PARBAT — NIGHT

The orange glow of kerosene lamps illuminates four tents pitched in a row, quaking in the wind.

HARRER'S VOICE resumes its narration.

> HARRER (V.O.)
> August 5, Camp Five. Some fierce storms have passed. My teammates are nervous about avalanches so we have been holed up for days.

INT. HARRER'S TENT — DUSK

Harrer writing in his diary, bored and disconsolate.

                    HARRER (V.O.)
          Aufschnaiter should take advantage of this lull in weather
          ...make high camp. But he disagrees with me...naturally.
          It seems the others don't mind sitting here, waiting, hop-
          ing, doing nothing. So much time to question oneself...
          is not good.

He turns a page of the diary, lingers on a PHOTOGRAPH taped to a page.
CLOSE ON PHOTO—Ingrid. She covers her large pregnant belly with her
hands; the strain in her smile is heartbreaking.

                    HARRER (V.O.)
          I am beginning to think this whole expedition was a
          mistake.

Harrer stares guiltily at the photo, then closes the diary.

EXT. CAMP SIX — DAWN

SHERPAS repair snow walls encircling their tiny encampment, trying to provide futile protection against the raging blizzard. It looks like the camp is
under siege.

EXT. CAMP SIX — DAWN

The whirlwind still rages. Hear a loud CRACK, the sound ricochets and
echoes across the mountain; explodes in a thundering RUMBLE. At the same
time, all the climbers and Sherpas bolt from their tents and look for protection. Through the haze of billowing spindrift, a massive AVALANCHE
roars down the mountainside like a furious white juggernaut. It narrowly
misses their camp.

EXT. SIX — DAY

See the Sherpas packing up gear, breaking camp. Nearby, Harrer and Aufschnaiter have locked horns in a bitter confrontation. Lobenhoffer and Chicken stand by, listening. All their nerves are stretched to the breaking point.

> AUFSCHNAITER
>
> —We're going down.

> HARRER
> *(points to Lobenhoffer and Chicken)*
>
> If they're afraid to climb in a storm, send them down to Camp Four and wait for me. I can make the summit on my own.
> *(pleading)*
> Give the best man his shot, Peter.

> CHICKEN
>
> I think he's trying to tell us he's the best man.

> HARRER
>
> That's not saying much, since I'm climbing with amateurs.
> *(fiercely)*
> I want that peak.

Fed up, Aufschnaiter turns to the others, who prepare to leave.

> AUFSCHNAITER
>
> We're going down now. As a team. And that's an order.

Aufschnaiter gestures for the team to follow him. Lobenhoffer and Chicken fall in line and begin the descent, followed by the Sherpas. Harrer stubbornly holds his ground until they're far out of sight. Then begins the long climb down the mountain all alone.

EXT. NANGA PARBAT — DAY

As the team retreats, MOVE WITH the Sherpas—CHANTING in Tibetan, passing a tinted photograph of the young Dalai Lama amongst themselves. Each Sherpa receives a blessing by pressing the photo to his forehead before passing it on.

EXT. NANGA PARBAT — DAY

Veils of snow obscure visibility. Alone, Harrer tries to follow a trail of bootprints quickly filling up with more snow.

He gives a start when a FIGURE emerges from the whiteness. A YOUNG SHERPA stands in front of him, smiling as he holds up his tinted photo of the Dalai Lama. He tries to press the photo to Harrer's forehead. Harrer demurs.

                    SHERPA
        Dalai Lama picture. Good protection.

                    HARRER
        It doesn't mean anything to me.

Insistent, the Sherpa grazes Harrer's forehead with the photo, then slips it inside Harrer's jacket pocket.

                    SHERPA
        Dalai Lama. Good protection.

EXT. BASE CAMP — DAY

Entering the camp, Harrer blinks in disbelief as scores of GURKHA SOL-DIERS emerge from behind rocks, training rifles on him. Perched awkwardly in the center of camp: Aufschnaiter, Lobenhoffer, and Chicken, handcuffed together. More Gurkha and British soldiers stream toward Harrer, led by a self-satisfied BRITISH OFFICER.

                    BRITISH OFFICER
        Let's hope Germany retreats from Poland as quickly as you

did from "your mountain," Herr Harrer. It might reduce your prison time.

Addled by the strenuous climb, Harrer gapes at the Officer.

> HARRER
>
> What is this?

> BRITISH OFFICER
>
> You are under arrest.

> HARRER
>
> What's the charge? Failure to summit?

> BRITISH OFFICER
>
> I'm afraid not.

Two Gurkhas yank Harrer's arms back, handcuff him.

> BRITISH OFFICER
>
> War has broken out between His Majesty's Government and Germany. All enemy aliens on British Empire soil are prisoners of war.

EXT. ROAD NEAR DEHRA DUN — DAY

Two Army trucks rumble up a dirt road toward a colossal prisoner-of-war camp nestled in the foothills. Seven great sections, each surrounded by double barbed wire fence, the whole camp enclosed by two more lines of wire entanglement. Gurkha patrols stationed everywhere.

EXT. BACK OF TRUCK — DAY

Approaching the forbidding-looking camp, Aufschnaiter, Chicken, and Lobenhoffer exchange despondent looks. Oblivious to his teammates, Harrer seems preoccupied, nervous. Then, with bewildering swiftness, he leaps up—vaults over the sidewalls of the truck and is gone.

EXT. ROAD — DAY

Landing with a heavy crash, Harrer smashes and reinjures his wounded leg. He winces in pain, gathers his knapsack with wrists still handcuffed together, and tries to make a run for it.

The army truck following them lurches to a stop. Gurkha soldiers race out and quickly overtake Harrer.

EXT. BACK OF TRUCK — DAY

Through the slats of the sidewalls, Aufschnaiter, Lobenhoffer, and Chicken peer out at the Gurkhas dragging Harrer's combative ass back to the truck.

EXT. PRISONER OF WAR CAMP — DAY

Holding Harrer tightly, the Gurkhas prod him toward the entrance gate manned by four SENTRIES.

HARRER'S NARRATION picks up.

> HARRER (V.O.)
> October 15, 1939. Reaching prison camp, I make a promise to myself...

Each step into the camp plunges Harrer deeper into despair. Then his gaze lights on something which lifts his spirits. He keeps staring straight ahead, at

POV — THE HIMALYAYAS: The mountains form a white-rimmed, rocky spine to the north.

> HARRER (V.O.)
> I will be lying beside Ingrid before summer solstice of the new year. The mountains are right in front of us. It will be easy to escape and get lost in them.

EXT. PLAINS NEAR PRISON CAMP — NIGHT

A TITLE appears: OCTOBER 2, 1940.

Harrer runs breathlessly in darkness. Suddenly, SIRENS BLARE. GUNFIRE explodes all around him. Harrer dives into a ditch as searchlights scan the darkness.

EXT. PRISON CAMP — NIGHT

Behind barbed wire, scores of German and Italian prisoners marvel at the sight of Gurkha soldiers dragging a torn-up, filthy Harrer back to the prison. He defiantly shoves a guard who is roughing him up.

HARRER'S V.O. continues.

> HARRER (V.O.)
> My fourth escape attempt brings me no closer to my goal.

EXT. PRISON CAMP YARD — NIGHT

As the Gurkhas lead Harrer toward a solitary confinement cell, prisoners bombard him with cheers.

> HARRER (V.O)
> All I have achieved is a certain dubious celebrity among the prisoners.

A PRISONER shouts out to Harrer.

> PRISONER
> How far did you get this time?

> HARRER
> Obviously not far enough.

EXT. SOLITARY CONFINEMENT CELL — NIGHT

An armed patrol outside a small, windowless hut.

INT. SOLITARY CONFINEMENT CELL — NIGHT

Harrer sits under a bare light bulb, counts his breath to stay collected, concentrating on something he holds. CLOSE ON object in Harrer's hand: It is his diary, opened to a calendar with the days checked off. He has a year of check marks filling the page, going from October 1939 to October 1940.

HARRER grabs a pencil stub, turns a page of the diary and pauses as he studies three words already written on the page, dated October 1939—one year earlier. CLOSE ON THREE WORDS: They are "My dearest Ingrid..."

HARRER poises the pencil stub above the page, tries to begin writing. Hesitates, uncertain what to say.

HARRER'S V.O. continues.

> HARRER (V.O.)
> If only my hand could express what is in my heart.

INT. PRISON BARRACKS — DAY

CLOSE ON LETTERS addressed to people in Germany, Austria, and Italy. WIDER TO REVEAL Aufschnaiter on his cot sorting through the letters. A monsoon pounds the barracks. Aufschnaiter sets the letters aside, resumes writing in a notebook. Nearby, Lobenhoffer on his cot is reading a book. Chicken is playing cards with two ITALIANS.

After a while, Harrer slowly approaches the three men's cots. Fidgets uncomfortably before speaking to Aufschnaiter.

HARRER

I understand the guards are mailing letters for you.

Aufschnaiter nods. Harrer pulls out a letter, offers it to him.

HARRER

Could you give them this?

CLOSE ON LETTER: It is addressed to Ingrid Harrer in Austria. Aufschnaiter nods, wordlessly sets it on the stack of other letters and glances at the others on their cots. Feeling unwelcome, Harrer starts to leave. Lobenhoffer quickly pipes up.

LOBENHOFFER

Hey, Heinrich, have you read this book? It was checked out to you.

Harrer casts a quick glance at the book in Lobenhoffer's hand.

HARRER

No.

LOBENHOFFER
(whispers conspiratorially)
Actually, we need to talk to you.

HARRER

What about?

Lobenhoffer reaches into the book, pulls out a fold-out map. CLOSE ON MAP: Of India, Tibet, and China, with routes marked in red ink. Chicken and the Italians move off the mattresses they're sitting on. Underneath are boxes. CLOSE ON BOXES: Filled with cans of food, bags of rice. CLOSE ON A BOX OF TOILET PAPER: Between each sheet are five-and ten-rupee notes. Harrer can't help but smile.

> HARRER
> Pretty impressive. When do you break out?

> LOBENHOFFER
> After monsoon season. And you?

Harrer shrugs evasively, unwilling to reveal too much. He carefully examines the map marking their escape route through the Himalayas, into Tibet, then China.

> HARRER
> I see you've chosen my route. Through Tibet.
> *(pauses)*
> So. Good luck.

> CHICKEN
> Would you like to come with us?

> HARRER
> *(stunned)*
> Why?

> CHICKEN
> After all, you're the authority on jailbreak around here.

> LOBENHOFFER
> We could benefit from your experience...

Exasperated, Aufschnaiter interrupts.

> AUFSCHNAITER
> Please stop this gruesome charade.

Every time you escape, Heinrich, patrols are doubled and tripled. It's making life difficult for the rest of us.

A pause as Harrer absorbs this. Then shrugs, unmoved.

                    HARRER
I prefer to travel on my own. But thanks for thinking of me.

EXT. PRISON YARD — DAY

As the monsoon drenches the camp, Harrer puts himself through the paces of a rigorous exercise regime, oblivious to the downpour.

EXT. PRISON MESS HALL — DAY

Hundreds of prisoners swill gruel at long tables. Harrer, by himself, eats quickly, never looking up. Aufschnaiter passes by, sets something beside Harrer's plate.

                    AUFSCHNAITER
The mailman has come.

Harrer glances down at a THICK ENVELOPE addressed to a guard at the camp. From Ingrid Harrer in Austria. Harrer picks up the envelope, overwhelmed. Looks around to thank Aufschnaiter. But he's already seated at another table with Chicken and Lobenhoffer.

INT. PRISON BARRACKS — DAY

Harrer lowers himself onto his cot. Opens the envelope and pulls out a SHEAF OF STAPLED PAPERS. A NOTE flutters to the ground. As he studies the sheaf of papers, his eagerness turns to confusion, then despair. CLOSE ON SHEAF OF PAPERS: They are divorce papers drafted by an Austrian lawyer.

Harrer reaches down, plucks the note from the floor. Reads it.

INGRID (O.S.)

Dear Heinrich, Please sign the enclosed divorce papers and send them to my lawyer. Horst and I intend to be married as soon as the divorce is finalized. As for your letter, yes, your son Rolf Harrer was born while you were climbing the mountain. He is now two years old and calls Horst "papa." When he is old enough, I will tell him his real father was lost in the Himalayas. It seems the kindest thing to say, considering you never wanted the child anyway. Needless to say, I have no intention of "resolving our differences," as you suggested. They were resolved the moment you left Austria. I am sorry you have been imprisoned in India and hope this dreadful war will soon be over, for everyone's sake. Ingrid.

EXT. PRISON CAMP — DAY

Rain still pours. Harrer steps out of the barracks and walks the perimeter of the yard. He stops, leans against the wall of barbed wire, holds onto it for support. It takes him a moment to realize he has grasped the wire so hard, his hands are bleeding. As if pulling himself from a trance, he steps back. Stares at the fence. Then hauls off and kicks it with all his strength—cursing and slamming his boots into the barbed wire until he's too drained to continue.

INT. PRISON BARRACKS — NIGHT

The ever-present SOUND of RAIN pummeling the metal barracks keeps most of the prisoners awake. Aufschnaiter, Chicken, and Lobenhoffer lie in their cots, whispering. Nearby, Harrer in his cot is as lifeless as a zombie. He closes his eyes, completely defeated.

INT. BARRACKS — MORNING

Harrer wakes from a deep sleep. It takes a moment to realize it is silent outside. No sound of rain. He looks over. Aufschnaiter, Lobenhoffer, and Chicken's cots are empty. Glancing down to the end of the barracks, he sees the three Germans and two Italians slinking out the door. Harrer remains motionless for a long time. Then quickly bolts up, grabs his rucksack and races toward the door.

EXT. BARRACKS — MORNING

Aufschnaiter, Lobenhoffer, and the Italians are already on the other side of a long wall of barbed wire which separates their section from another one housing more prisoners. Chicken slips then through a breach in the fence, replaces the tampered wire. The five men disappear into a hut. A moment later, Harrer appears in front of the barbed wire. Pulls back the tampered section and wriggles to the adjoining partition.

INT. HUT — DAY

Aufschnaiter, Lobenhoffer, Chicken, and the two Italians are quickly undressing. Aufschnaiter opens a jar of shoe polish, dips a cloth inside when the door opens. All of them give a start when Harrer skulks inside.

                    HARRER
        I'm coming with you.

                    AUFSCHNAITER
        Oh.

He looks so demoralized, Aufschnaiter takes pity on him. Tosses him a robe. Catching the robe, Harrer suddenly realizes how they're planning to escape. He shakes his head, always the expert.

                    HARRER
        In my humble opinion, this will never work—

                    AUFSCHNAITER
        Then since you're so humble, we won't ask your opinion.

EXT. MAIN GATE — DAY

Sentries stand guard at the entrance, which is separated from the rest of the camp by yet another barbed wire enclosure.

EXT. BARBED WIRE — DAY

Slinking toward the barbed wire, see Harrer and the three other Germans dressed up as an Indian repair crew; they wear white *dhotis*, heads wrapped in turbans, faces stained dark with shoe polish. The two Italians wear English officers' uniforms. Harrer seems almost embarrassed to be attempting such an ignominious escape. Keeps shaking his head as the group creeps over to a breach in the fence. One by one, they slip into the area leading to the main gate.

EXT. MAIN GATE — DAY

From where they stand, it is about three hundred yards to the main gate. They slowly walk toward the gate in unison. The "English officers" carry rolls of blueprints under their arms and swing swagger canes. The "Indians" carry long rolls of barbed wire and tar pots.

They pass by a GURKHA SOLDIER, who doesn't pay them heed. As they continue walking, Harrer is stunned that they can pass through the yard undetected. Only a few feet from the main gate, the SERGEANT MAJOR whisks past on his bicycle. Quickly, the "officers" turn to give a close inspection to the barbed wire near the gate, hiding their faces. The "Indians" pretend to be occupied with their tar pots. All hold their breath as the Sergeant Major circles round them, then shoots over to the SENTRIES at the main gate and confers with them. After a moment, he rides off. Aufschnaiter nods for the group to continue. And they start walking.

With Harrer dragging in the rear, the five men approach the gate. The sentries are whispering. Trepidatiously, the men come abreast of the sentries— who are still locked in conversation. The sentries swiftly shift their atten-

102

tion to the men. An excruciating moment of recognition passes, then with curt formality, the sentries salute the "English officers," embarrassed to have been caught loafing on the job.

In groups of two, the prisoners step out of the main gate. Harrer is the last to exit the camp. As he steps into freedom, he pauses, waiting for the curtain to drop. Nothing happens. He seems amazed that the escape was so easy. Up ahead, Aufschnaiter shoots him a wry, triumphant smile.

EXT. BUSHES IN FOOTHILLS — DAY

The prison camp lies a safe distance away. In the bushes, the men strip off their Indian robes and Army uniforms. Underneath they are wearing khakis, knapsacks strapped to their backs. They toss their costumes into the bushes. Harrer is first to finish.

                         HARRER
        I'm going off on my own.

The others stand there in stunned silence as Harrer spins around and starts running. As he disappears into the scrub, the WAIL of a SIREN rises from the camp below. With breakneck speed, the four men split into teams of two and start running.

EXT. JUMNA AND AGLAR RIVERS — DUSK TO NIGHT

As the terrain breaks into jungle, Harrer runs alongside the Jumna River, never breaking his stride. He reaches the Aglar, a smaller tributary.

A SERIES OF SHOTS: Harrer wades across the Aglar ... reaches the river bank ... runs until the path is blocked by jungle and rocks ... jumps back into the river ... wades across ...

EXT. AGLAR VALLEY — DUSK

Covered with scratches and bruises, Harrer sets camp between two boulders on the riverbed. Painfully lifts his foot: the soles of his tennis shoes have worn through.

He reaches inside his knapsack and takes out his diary, starts to note down the terrain and distance he has covered. Turns a page and stops writing. Something on this new page gives him pause.

His VOICE NARRATES what is written on the page.

> HARRER (V.O.)
> First escape from prison camp...November 18, 1939...Rolf Harrer three-and-a-half months old.
> *(pauses)*
> My thirtieth birthday, July 6, 1941...Rolf Harrer...exactly one year, eleven months, and twenty-six days...Last escape from Dehra Dun...Rolf Harrer...

The low melody of a LULLABY is heard.

INT. ROOM IN POTALA — DAY

The same LULLABY plays. Ear pressed close to his music box, the Dalai Lama, now eight years old, listens to the music, bewitched. A HAND reaches down, closes the box. The young boy tries to conceal his disappointment as one of his tutors, LING RINPOCHE, takes the box away. Ling Rinpoche looks like a giant Tibetan teddy bear. The Dalai Lama's other tutor, sinewy and stern TRIJANG RINPOCHE, enters the room with an elderly monk: THE MASTER OF ROBES. The Master of Robes is carrying a gold silk ceremonial robe for the Dalai Lama. The deep bellow of HORNS is heard.

EXT. POTALA — DAY

In an immense courtyard, a procession is gathering. Lamas consecrate a yellow palanquin; monks hoist tall yellow parasols over pallid nobles in brocades and furs.

Enormous monk bodyguards called GYE OKS hold back a crowd. The Gye Oks wear padded robes and wield big sticks. Near a row of horses outfitted in jeweled caparisons stand the Dalai Lama's Mother and Father. Beside them is the Regent, TATHAG RINPOCHE. In his early 60s, Tathag is a stern, censorious man given to erratic outbursts of bombast. The Dalai Lama's parents—and entire crowd in courtyard—turn to a curtained doorway as long silver horns are blown by young monks. The crowd hushes. Preceded by ten Gye Oks, flanked by his two tutors, the Dalai Lama is led outdoors, wearing the gold silk ceremonial robe. As he is escorted to his palanquin, he passes his parents, who are still bowing. The Dalai Lama lightly touches his mother's head, blessing her. She does not dare look up to meet his eyes. Leading him away, the Gye Oks help the Dalai Lama into the yellow palanquin. Once inside, a curtain is drawn.

His mother gazes over at the sedan chair, unable to see her son behind the curtain.

EXT. COUNTRYSIDE — DAY

The procession of monks and nobles on horseback, with the Regent, tutors, and Dalai Lama's parents riding in front of the palanquin, moves quickly up a dirt road, passing more people lined alongside the route. The Tibetans on the roadside bow and prostrate as the palanquin passes.

CLOSE ON CURTAIN OF PALANQUIN: A SMALL HAND pulls back the curtain, just a hair. The Dalai Lama peeks out at a world that cannot look him in the eye.

EXT. UTTAR KASHI — NIGHT

In the dead of night, Harrer staggers into an ancient temple town etched into a mountainside. Narrow, labyrinthine streets glow dimly with candle-light from temples. Harrer has to leap into shadow to avoid being spotted by some PRIESTS; slinks into one of the temples to elude more people coming down another street.

INT. KALI TEMPLE — NIGHT

In the center of temple is an altar with the ferocious-looking, bloodstained Kali idol. Heaped near it are offerings: flowers, sindoor powder, fruit, incense, and bowls of water; a dead chicken is draped at the foot of the idol. Starving, Harrer feverishly gulps water and rice from the offering bowls. Dumps coins into his pocket. Grabs the dead chicken. Turning to leave, he sees some HINDUS entering the temple. He flies past them, screaming like a demon to scare them away.

EXT. MOUNTAINSIDE — NIGHT

High above, a full moon casts a silvery light as a lone SHADOW combs the mountain. Coming close to an outcropping of huge boulders, the SHADOW pauses, slowly tiptoes forward, peers behind the boulders: the embers of a fire still glow. Chicken bones are strewn by the campfire. Nearby, Harrer on hands and knees is heaving up the last bit of tainted meat. He hears the RUSTLE of FOOTSTEPS, panics, crawls painfully toward a rock when a SMALL TIN CONTAINER hits the ground. Dumbfounded, Harrer reaches for the TIN. Is even more astounded to discover it's MAGNESIA TABLETS. He peers up as the SHADOW slowly emerges into moonlight to reveal PETER AUFSCHNAITER. Like Harrer, Aufschnaiter is filthy and very thin.

> AUFSCHNAITER
> Take two and sleep it off. I'll send you a bill in the morning.

                    HARRER
                    (groans)
What are you doing here?

                    AUFSCHNAITER
I missed you so much, Heinrich, I thought I'd stop by
for a visit.

Harrer collapses to the ground, miserable.

                    HARRER
Where are the others?

                    AUFSCHNAITER
The Italians were caught outside Nelang. Lutz and Hans
took ill and had to turn back.

Gulping two magnesia tablets, Harrer weakly stifles a gag.

                    HARRER
I'm sorry to hear that.

                    AUFSCHNAITER
I'm sure you're heartbroken.
                    (exhausted)
May I impose upon your generous nature and camp here
tonight?

                    HARRER
Please . . . be my guest.

                    AUFSCHNAITER
Very gracious of you.

Aufschnaiter rolls out a tattered blanket, wraps himself in it.

EXT. CAMPSITE — MORNING

Harrer wakes up as Aufschnaiter pours himself a bowl of cereal, adds water and sugar. Then takes a packet of dried beef from his knapsack.

> HARRER
> What else do you have in there? A ten-piece orchestra?

Aufschnaiter doesn't respond, quickly eats his cereal. Harrer finds a stale, broken cracker in his pack and nibbles on it, coveting Aufschnaiter's breakfast. They eat in silence for a while.

> AUFSCHNAITER
> You might be interested to know...I've heard the Japanese have retreated all the way to Shanghai. Even if you reach the Chinese border, you may never catch up with them.

> HARRER
> I don't care if the Japanese get repelled all the way back to Tokyo.

> AUFSCHNAITER
> You will if you plan to get back to Austria.

> HARRER
> But I don't.

> AUFSCHNAITER
> You don't what?

> HARRER
> Plan to go back..."home."

AUFSCHNAITER
(surprised)

Why not?

HARRER

No particular reason.
(feigning boredom)
But when you get there, tell my wife that two years in prison
camp was roughly equivalent to four years of marriage. And
I'm glad to be free of both.

His bitterness gives Aufschnaiter pause; he hesitates before speaking.

AUFSCHNAITER

I'm not going back either. At least until this shameful war
is over.

Now it's Harrer's turn to be surprised.

HARRER

Where are you headed?

AUFSCHNAITER

Tibet. Then on to China. I'll try to find work in Peking.
(cautiously)
What about you?

Harrer shrugs—has no idea where he's headed. Trying to appear casual, he
covertly studies the ample supply of food Aufschnaiter is carrying.

HARRER

By my calculations, the Chinese border is 2,058 kilometers
away. And the Tibetan border is sixty-eight kilometers.
(shakes his head, points to Aufschnaiter's pack)

That's a long way to travel. You'd move a lot faster with the two of us carrying that pack.

Enjoying himself immensely, Aufschnaiter chuckles, fully aware of what Harrer is attempting to negotiate.

                    AUFSCHNAITER
It's full of food.
                        (grinning)
Mine.

                    HARRER
That goes without saying.

There's a moment's pause as Harrer tries to appear cautious and somber.

                    HARRER
Those mountains farther up are nasty. We've got glaciers to cross, and if we rope up together, we'll stay alive.

                    AUFSCHNAITER
Considering your performance last time we roped up, I think I'm safer without you.

Harrer smiles thinly, stands up, preparing to leave.

                    AUFSCHNAITER
But I think you're wrong about that Tibetan border calculation. By my measurements, it's sixty-five kilometers.

Harrer smirks with satisfaction, unaware that Aufschnaiter is throwing him a bone.

                    HARRER
Are you willing to wager a kilo of food on that?

AUFSCHNAITER
(can't resist)
All you've got are some stale crackers, Heinrich.

Harrer crosses his arms over his chest, regaining his treasured arrogance.

HARRER
That's true. But I'm right. And I'll win.

EXT. MOUNTAIN — DUSK

From a distance, see the two men reach the tree line; they emerge from a sparse alpine forest into a barren, moonlike landscape... CLOSER ON HARRER AND AUFSCHNAITER: At higher altitude, in the middle of lunar emptiness, they pass a lone campsite with fire-blackened stones... set around it, larger rocks with the mantra "OM MANI PADME HUM" painted on the sides .... The earth beneath them rumbles, the wind whines like a sentient thing; the sense of awe and excitement grows more visible as they push onward to a new world.

EXT. MOUNTAIN TRAIL — DAY

Nearing a pass at the top of mountain, they hear loud SHOUTING in guttural Asian.

VOICES (O.S.)
(in Tibetan)
The Gods are victorious!

Looking around, they see nothing. They keep walking. Much farther ahead, they begin to make out a small caravan of TIBETAN NOMADS descending with a flock of sheep. The two men continue up .... After a time, they cross paths with the nomads. Slanted, mistrustful brown eyes glare at them from dust-coated faces. Matted hair plaited in braids to the waist, studded with turquoise and coral jewelry. Some of the nomads spin prayer wheels or twirl *malas*—rosaries—through their fingers.

> HARRER
> (*meekly*)
> Hello.

Glowering, the nomads raise two fingers above their heads—making devil's horns. They HISS loudly, trying to drive the evil spirits away.

> NOMADS
> (*in Tibetan*)
> Devils.

Harrer and Aufschnaiter skitter up the path, anxious to get away.

EXT. TSANGCHOKLA PASS — DAY

Hundreds of faded red, yellow, blue, and green prayer flags flutter in the wind. Perched at 17,200 feet, they stand at the gateway to Tibet. Aufschnaiter points to the sprawling tableland below.

> AUFSCHNAITER
> There it is. Tibet.

Harrer's busy making calculations in his notebook.

> HARRER
> Exactly sixty-eight kilometers, by the way.

> AUFSCHNAITER
> Congratulations. Unfortunately, you've eaten all your
> winnings.

EXT. TIBETAN VALLEY — DAY

Overhanging rock walls flank the valley. The landscape is barren, desolate:

monochromatic brown against a brilliant blue sky. Whitewashed *stupas*—reliquaries—are built into the rock face, making it look like a work of supernatural sculpture. Harrer and Aufschnaiter inch up a narrow path.

HARRER'S NARRATION comes up over this image.

> HARRER (V.O.)
> Tibet ... "the roof of the world." It feels as though we have ascended a medieval stone fortress ... towering above the center of Asia. This is the highest country on earth, and the most isolated.

EXT. TIBETAN VALLEY — DAY

Trudging up a dusty road, Harrer and Aufschnaiter HEAR the TINKLING OF BELLS. TWO MEN on small ponies trot toward them, bells fastened to the ponies' bridles. The men are small, like the ponies; their embroidered brocade robes and fur caps only add to the toylike impression. As they come to a stop, Harrer whispers to Aufschnaiter.

> HARRER
> When you don't speak the language, it's best to smile and say "yes."

Aufschnaiter nods thoughtfully, then turns to the men. And proceeds to speak in flawless Tibetan.

> AUFSCHNAITER
> *(in Tibetan)*
> We have come from India.

Harrer's mouth drops. Quietly relishing his moment of triumph, Aufschnaiter smiles.

> AUFSCHNAITER
> Amazing what you learn in prison, isn't it?

The two Tibetans murmur to themselves, then point to the mountains.

> MAN #1
> (*in Tibetan*)

Get out. Now.

> MAN #2
> (*in Tibetan*)

Foreigners are not permitted in Tibet.

The two men roost on their ponies, blocking the path. Harrer signals to Aufschnaiter, who follows as Harrer walks brazenly past the men, ignoring them. The men kick their ponies and trot up a few feet ahead, blocking their path.

> MAN #1
> (*in Tibetan*)

Out...out...foreigners not allowed without permits.

Harrer rolls his eyes and walks up to the man and his pony. Without further ado, he pushes them out of his way. Then marches over to the second man and his pony and shoves them aside too. Thoroughly offended and intimidated, the two men retreat and gallop off. Harrer turns back to Aufschnaiter.

> HARRER

No translation needed.

EXT. VILLAGE — DAY

Approaching a small village, Harrer and Aufschnaiter see a line of VILLA-GERS come out to greet them, until the entrance is blocked with people. They slowly begin to CLAP their hands together as Harrer and Aufschnaiter walk past. Harrer waves to them, feeling cocky.

> HARRER

Some people are glad to see us.

AUFSCHNAITER

Don't let it go to your head, Heinrich. When Tibetans clap
hands, it means they're driving out evil forces.

The CLAPPING is louder, more insistent. They take a few more steps, are
accosted by a dour, authoritative MONK OFFICIAL. Both men promptly bow
and grovel.

AUFSCHNAITER
(in Tibetan)
Where can we get travel permits and food?

MONK OFFICIAL

You talk to Garpon.

INT. HOUSE — DAY

The Monk Official sends the attendant to fetch the Garpon. He stays with
Harrer and Aufschnaiter, keeping careful watch over them as they examine
the room. There is the ubiquitous altar, with a Buddha statue, copies of
Buddhist scriptures, and a small *stupa*. Placed all around the altar are tinted
photos of the young Dalai Lama. Some of his predecessor, the Great
Thirteenth. Next to the Thirteenth's picture is some kind of official
government PROCLAMATION in Tibetan. The Monk Official picks up the
proclamation to show them.

MONK OFFICIAL
The final testament of Great Thirteenth Dalai Lama.
(points to picture of the Thirteenth)
It is prophecy. It says . . .
(reads slowly and haltingly)
"It may happen that here, in Tibet, religion and . . . government . . . will be attacked by outside forces. Unless we can
guard our own country, monks and their . . . monasteries will

be destroyed . . . the lands and property of government officials will be seized. The Dalai Lama and all the . . . revered holders of the faith will disappear and become nameless."

(sets it down)

Now you understand why we are not welcome to foreigners here.

HARRER

But we haven't come to disturb any—

At that moment, the GARPON and his AGENT enter the room. Harrer recoils —they are the same two men Harrer and Aufschnaiter pushed off the road farther back. The Garpon and his Agent regard the two men with silent disdain. Reaching into his pocket, Harrer steps forward, bowing humbly.

HARRER

Your Eminence, I have a special offering for you.

GARPON

You have nothing I want.

Harrer removes something from his pocket, gravely presents it. It is the tinted photo of the Dalai Lama, given to him by the Sherpa on Nanga Parbat.

HARRER

Long live His Holiness the Dalai Lama.

EXT. VILLAGE — DAY

At the entrance to the village, the Garpon drapes white scarves—*khatas*—around Harrer and Aufschnaiter's necks, a Tibetan tradition for honoring arrivals and departures. Standing beside them are two burly GUIDES.

GARPON

Thank you for the picture. Now go back to India.

EXT. ROAD — DAY

Harrer and Aufschnaiter bristle at being hemmed in on both sides by their vigilant Guides. The two Austrians quicken their pace; the Guides keep up. They slow down; the Guides follow suit.

Resume HARRER'S NARRATION.

HARRER (V.O.)

Two days into Tibet's western frontier, and we are given the bum's rush. Our guards have express orders to escort us to the Indian border, some forty kilometers away. Though the Tibetans call themselves a peaceful people, the guides are allowed to shoot us if we escape.

EXT. VILLAGE AND BAZAAR — DAY

Outside a small village is a sprawling nomad's market. Yaks, sheep, and goats graze in the field in front of the market. At individual stalls, NOMADS from different regions sell grain, butter, animals. Household articles are in abundance: needles, aluminum pots and pans, yarn, ornaments.

Harrer, Aufschnaiter, and their two Guides approach the bazaar.

EXT. BAZAAR — DAY

As they enter, all the nomads stop their business to gape at the foreigners. One by one, they open their mouths and stick out their tongues. Harrer and Aufschnaiter's Guides respond by sticking out their tongues, too.

                        AUFSCHNAITER
Must mean hello.

                        HARRER
Just so long as they don't try to kiss me.

Everyone remains frozen, tongues extended. Waiting. Harrer and Aufschnaiter gamely stick out their tongues and the entire marketplace resumes business as usual. With their Guards closely tailing them, they wander past stalls where dust-covered nomads ply their goods. They reach a stall where there is a brisk trade in butter and barley grains. Harrer turns to Aufschnaiter and whispers.

                        HARRER
We need to stock up. I'm tapped out.

                        AUFSCHNAITER
Don't look at me.

Harrer points to a watch Aufschnaiter is wearing.

AUFSCHNAITER

Not negotiable. My father gave it to me when I climbed
Mont Blanc.

HARRER

Everyone's climbed Mont Blanc, Peter.
(*reprovingly*)
If I had a watch like that, I'd trade it.

Aufschnaiter stiffens with resentment, then removes his watch and com-
mences trading with the vendor. Their guides start digging through stacks
of dirty clothes in the stall. One of the guides tries on a jacket and hat.
When Harrer sees him, he does a double take. It is a stained, green Chinese
People's Liberation Army jacket. And the green PLA cap with red star.
Confused, Harrer turns to the vendor.

HARRER

Where did you get that jacket?

VENDOR

Amdo. North Tibet. Communism soldiers come from
China. Very nice. They give money, food. Very nice,
Communism soldiers.

Harrer shakes his head, then turns and watches their Guard parade around
in the Chinese jacket, quite pleased with it. Struck by a plan, Harrer sidles
up to Aufschnaiter, whispers in his ear.

HARRER

Want to see how quickly we can get rid of these guards?

Then Harrer turns to their guides.

HARRER

You like military uniforms? We have some German
Army boots.

While Aufschnaiter translates in Tibetan, Harrer holds up their spiky metal crampons. The Guides have never seen anything so bizarre looking in their lives.

HARRER

Go ahead. Try them on.

Again, Aufschnaiter translates into Tibetan. As a bemused crowd gathers, the Guide wearing the jacket lifts his foot and Harrer straps on a crampon. Aufschnaiter leans down and straps on the other guide's crampons. They twist leather shoe strings around their feet to secure them. More onlookers press forward, murmuring. When both Guides have the crampons securely fastened, Harrer stands up.

HARRER

Now I'll show you how German soldiers march.

Harrer proceeds to march a few steps doing a demented goose step. With the rapt crowd egging them on, the Guides follow Harrer and religiously imitate everything he does. But it is hard work negotiating in the crampons; they nearly stumble and fall. As Aufschnaiter slinks up beside Harrer, Harrer turns to the guides.

HARRER

And now we'll show you how German soldiers run.

In a flash, Harrer and Aufschnaiter take off running. At first, the crowd thinks it's still part of the demonstration. The Guides in crampons try to run and fall flat on their faces. Harrer and Aufschnaiter fly through the bazaar into the nearby village.

EXT. VILLAGE — DAY

Running as fast as they can, they scramble up steep passageways leading directly onto the mountain.

EXT. MOUNTAIN — DAY

From a distance, see the two men race up a narrow hairpin trail toward a plateau at the top.

EXT. PLATEAU — LATE DAY

As the dusk sky turns blood red, they reach the plateau. Harrer drops to his knees, panting. Greedily opens his knapsack and gulps water from a canteen. Aufschnaiter flops down beside him. They lie there stupefied, trying to catch their breath.

> HARRER
> See if they're following us.

> AUFSCHNAITER
> You go.

Harrer drags himself to his feet, staggers over to the edge of plateau. Beyond, the Tibetan plain spreads out as vast and wide as an ocean. Harrer slowly wanders the perimeter of the plateau, scouts for their Guides.

Aufschnaiter, lying on the ground, turns his head, his eyes only inches from Harrer's open knapsack. A few provisions spill out. Aufschnaiter sees something shiny inside the pack, tilts his head closer to get a better look, dismayed by what Harrer has hidden. He reaches in, pulls out three WATCHES tied together with a rubber band, and Harrer's gold wedding band. Aufschnaiter scrambles to his feet and marches over to Harrer, who's still at the edge of plateau.

EXT. EDGE OF PLATEAU — LATE DAY

Harrer turns when he hears footsteps. Faces Aufschnaiter.

> AUFSCHNAITER
> Know what time it is?

Harrer is shocked to see mild-mannered Aufschnaiter flushing with rage. Aufschnaiter hurls the watches toward Harrer.

                    AUFSCHNAITER
Refresh my memory. What did you say at the bazaar
back there?
                        (livid)
"If I had a watch like that, I'd trade it." You don't have one,
you cheap lying bastard, you have three!

Harrer straightens up, unruffled.

                    HARRER
You have a problem, Peter?

                    AUFSCHNAITER
—You think I'm so happy to travel with you, I should foot
the bill? You're such a big man you don't need to contribute?

                    HARRER
                (dangles the watches)
This is junk. From some Italian prisoners.

                    AUFSCHNAITER
I don't give a shit! Haven't you ever heard of a principle?

                    HARRER
                (derisively)
Go ahead. Take one. And keep your principles.

Handing Aufschnaiter the packet of watches, Harrer starts moving, tries to put some distance between them.

                    AUFSCHNAITER
Look at you. Caught being a selfish prick and you're gloating.

HARRER

You sound like an old woman, Peter. What do you want
me to do?

AUFSCHNAITER

Try apologizing. Try feeling a little remorse. If all else fails,
try wiping that smirk off your face.

HARRER
(pushes him)

Take a watch and shut up! I don't need another boring
sermon from some frustrated, glorified tour guide.

Aufschnaiter spins around, takes a few steps, and grabs his knapsack.

AUFSCHNAITER

No wonder you're always alone. Who could stand your
miserable company?

Tossing the watches back to Harrer, Aufschnaiter turns and stalks down the
trail. Watching him descend, Harrer shrugs his shoulders: no big loss. Then,
as Aufschnaiter gets farther away, Harrer goes slack with remorse. Abruptly
grabs his pack and streaks like a bullet down the center of the hill, bypass-
ing the switchbacks until he is gaining on Aufschnaiter.

EXT. HILL — LATE DAY

Reaching Aufschaniter, Harrer pauses to catch his breath. Cautiously
extends his hand. In it are the watches and Harrer's wedding ring.

HARRER

Please take them.
(pauses, embarrassed)
It was wrong to hide them.

It's probably the first time in his life he's admitted he was wrong. Aufschnaiter accepts the watches but removes the wedding ring.

                    AUFSCHNAITER
Keep this.

                    HARRER
No. I didn't deserve it, either.

He shoots such a plangent look of remorse, Aufschnaiter is oddly moved, quietly accepts the ring.

EXT. VALLEY — DUSK

As night settles in, the two men descend the remainder of the trail together and strike out into the valley.

EXT. NIGHT SKY — LATER

The sky is ablaze with thousands of stars.

                    HARRER (O.S.)
...He's about three and a half years old now. Pretty soon, she'll tell him I got lost in the Himalayas. So he'll have a dead father. Which is fine with me.

EXT. CAMPSITE — NIGHT

Harrer and Aufschnaiter lie wrapped in their blankets.

                    AUFSCHNAITER
Why?

                    HARRER
Better a dead father than a lousy father.

A long silence as they stare up at the sky.

AUFSCHNAITER
(pauses)
Write him a letter and tell him you're alive.

INT. STOREROOM — DAY

CLOSE ON A POSTCARD of the Arc de Triomphe in Paris. A CHILD'S HAND comes into FRAME, holds the postcard in front of a candle. WIDER TO REVEAL a ten-year-old Dalai Lama placing postcards from Europe and America over a rectangular hole in a blackboard; a candle behind the postcard illuminates it as if on a slide projector. It's a show-and-tell to explain the Western world to the Dalai Lama's elderly SWEEPER — room attendant. The two of them are in a dusty, cavernous storeroom in the Potala. Gifts, toys, fabric are piled up in storeroom, along with stacks and stacks of books. Perched by a half-open door, the Sweeper claps appreciatively as the Dalai Lama shows him a postcard of the Statue of Liberty. Then he peeks out the door and balks.

Outside, in the hallway, the Dalai Lama's tutors—Ling Rinpoche and Trijang Rinpoche—are searching for His Holiness. The Sweeper puts his finger to his lips, signaling to the Dalai Lama, who quickly extinguishes the candle. As the room fades into darkness, HARRER'S VOICE comes up.

> HARRER (V.O.)
> Dear Rolf Harrer, I am a person you don't know.
> A man you've never met . . .

EXT. TIBETAN PLATEAU — DAY

Rimmed by the Himalayas, a brilliant turquoise lake glistens in the high plateau. Harrer and Aufschnaiter stand at the water's edge.

> HARRER (V.O.)
> But you are someone who occupies my mind . . . and my heart . . . in this distant land where I've gone.

EXT. VALLEY — DAY

Hiking through a valley, clouds cast massive shadows over the arid table-land. The omnipresent, snowcapped Himalayas in the distance.

> HARRER (V.O.)
> If you can imagine a hidden place, tucked safely away from the world . . . concealed by walls of high, snow-capped mountains . . . a place rich with all the strange beauty of your nighttime dreams . . .

A rainbow appears over a mountain ridge.

HARRER (V.O.)

Then you know where I am.

EXT. MOUNT KAILAS — DAY

Rising in isolated splendor, Kailas is the most sacred of Tibetan mountains. Along the path, rock cairns are erected—huge heaps of stone, some towering over the throngs of devout PILGRIMS approaching the mountain. Most are performing full-length prostrations.

HARRER (V.O.)

In the country where I'm traveling—Tibet—people believe if they walk long distances to holy places...it purifies the bad deeds they've committed...

EXT. MOUNTAINSIDE — DAY

Perspiring in the summer heat, the two of them trudge up a trail. A YOUNG MONK comes running down a hill, straight toward them, his robes flying open like a big red parachute. The monk stops. And holds out two small dried apricots as gifts for Harrer and Aufschnaiter.

HARRER (V.O.)

...They believe the more difficult the journey, the greater the depth of purification.

EXT. FROZEN WATERFALL — DAY

In the dead of winter, Harrer reaches out to help Aufschnaiter. The two of them are roped together, carefully ascending an icefall.

EXT. FIELD — DAY

Harrer and Aufschnaiter sneak through a grove of poplar trees on the edge of a barley field. In the field, a long procession of monks carrying Buddhist scriptures blesses the spring crops.

HARRER (V.O.)

I've been walking from one faraway place to the next for many years—as long as you have lived. I have seen seasons change across these high plateaus...

EXT. ROAD — DAY

A dark storm cloud opens up, spilling down snow on Harrer and Aufschnaiter staggering up a road. They numbly hold out their hands to beg when a yak caravan passes.

HARRER (V.O.)

...In this place where time stands still, it seems that everything is moving. Including me.

EXT. MOUNTAIN PASS — DAY

Total whiteness. Then, like two shadow puppets, Harrer and Aufschnaiter emerge from the veil of a blizzard. Beards dripping icicles, eyelashes frozen together.

HARRER (V.O.)

I can't say I know where I'm going. Nor whether my bad deeds can be purified...there are so many things I've done which I regret.

They reach the top of a pass and stare with glazed eyes at

POV — THE CHANGTANG: There is no descent; the frozen plateau of rock and salt deposits in front of them stretches out to what seems like infinity.

AUFSCHNAITER slumps to the ground in misery. His shredded boots expose blackened, bloody toes. Frostbite has set in; he's too exhausted to continue.

Harrer quickly removes his still fairly intact boots. Hands them to Aufschnaiter.

                    HARRER
      Here. Wear these.

EXT. CHANGTANG — DAY

From a distance, see Harrer holding Aufschnaiter by the waist as they continue onward.

                    HARRER (V.O.)
      But when I come to a full stop, I hope you will understand
      that the distance between us is not as great as it seems....
      With deep affection, your father...Heinrich Harrer.

EXT. HILL — DAY

Stumbling down a slope, Harrer and Aufschnaiter hear the sound of
CHANTING and BELLS RINGING. Up ahead, clouds break. Like a mirage, a
group of PILGRIMS appears through the haze, coming toward them.

EXT. PILGRIM CARAVAN — DAY

Looking like two skeletal wraiths, Harrer and Aufschnaiter race toward the
pilgrims. Several of the pilgrims are wearing ratty PLA jackets and caps; all
take pity on the two men, give them food, money.

                    HARRER
      Where are you going?

                    PILGRIM #1
      Lhasa...holy city Lhasa...

                    HARRER
      We go, too.

                    PILGRIM #2
      Impossible. Foreigners not allowed in Lhasa.

With his last shred of dignity, Aufschnaiter pulls a dog-eared inventory of his first-aid kit from a pocket—with its official-looking red cross on top. Presents it to the nomads.

AUFSCHNAITER

We have permission to enter Lhasa. Yes, permission.

Grabbing the inventory, the nomads' eyes widen and they pull Harrer and Aufschnaiter into their midst.

EXT. ROOF OF POTALA — DAY

The Dalai Lama is poised on the edge of roof, face pressed to a telescope. Staring fixedly.

POV — THROUGH TELESCOPE:

Streaming from all directions, hordes of pilgrims converge on the main road to the city.

EXT. PILGRIM CARAVAN — DAY

Harrer and Aufschnaiter moving with pilgrims—drawn like magnets through the verdant Kyichu River valley.

HARRER'S NARRATION over this.

> HARRER (V.O.)
> The Forbidden City of Lhasa is as difficult a goal as Mecca ... and precisely as attractive because it is closed to all foreigners.

At the same time, a loud GASP resonates from the crowd. All eyes aimed straight ahead at POV—THE GOLDEN ROOFS OF THE POTALA: gleaming in the clear mountain air.

> HARRER (V.O.)
> Only a few outsiders had penetrated its mysteries.

EXT. ROAD TO LHASA — DAY

The road teeming with more people—travelers, traders, nobles. Many inch their way toward the Holy City doing full length prostrations. Harrer and Aufschnaiter hide behind the masses, worried about two SENTRIES guarding the gates to the city.

The sentries scan the crowds for foreigners. Let two filthy pilgrims—Harrer and Aufschnaiter—enter the Forbidden City.

EXT. LHASA — DAY

Towering over the ancient city like a stone sentinel is the Potala. Below, the route from the entrance gates into the heart of the city is bordered by walls of polished bronze prayer wheels. Monks file past, adroitly giving each wheel a spin. On the dirt roads, horse-drawn carts teeter past, laden with silks and spices. Imperious NOBLEWOMEN in brocades and furs, wearing elaborate and tall headdresses, haggle with MUSLIM MERCHANTS over the price of exotic perfumes.

Harrer and Aufschnaiter wander through the sacred city in a stupor, overwhelmed with emotion at reaching this most inner of sanctums. They pass an open market where flies have settled like a mist over slabs of bloody yak meat. They pass a stand where a VENDOR wraps bricks of hard, rancid butter in old newspaper. Harrer spots a newspaper headline and gasps.

                              HARRER
     Is it over?

Aufschnaiter watches in confusion as Harrer reaches over and yanks the newspaper from the stand. It is an old English language edition of the *Indian Standard*.

CLOSE ON NEWSPAPER: On the front page, pictures of Allied troops storming the beachhead at Normandy. The headline: D-DAY FOR ALLIED TROOPS. The date—June, 1944.

HARRER AND AUFSCHNAITER lean down to gape at such incongruous news from the outside world.

                           AUFSCHNAITER
                              (sadly)
     No, it's not over.

EXT. ESTATE — DAY

Like somnambulists, they drift aimlessly down a narrow street, pause outside the gates of an affluent estate. Beyond the gates, a sprawling garden lies fallow in winter. A spindly old SERVANT WOMAN brings out dog food for two small Lhasa Apsos, sets the bowls in garden. Harrer and Aufschnaiter wait until she disappears, then creep into the garden.

EXT. GARDEN — DAY

Crouching down, they stuff the dogs' food into their mouths. Suddenly, the Servant Woman barges out of the house and clobbers them with a broom.

> SERVANT WOMAN
> (in Tibetan)
> Filthy dogs! Thieves! Go away! No food!

Through the trees, see TSARONG, a kindly, dignified man in his sixties, rushing to the men's rescue.

> TSARONG
> (in Tibetan)
> Tashi, please. Stop.

The Servant Woman—TASHI—immediately stops beating the men when Tsarong appears. Tsarong's eyes soften at the sight of the men's bloody, blistered feet, threadbare clothes, emaciated bodies.

> TSARONG
> You are invited to stay for lunch if you like.

Tashi drops her mouth in horror.

> HARRER
> Thank you. We like it very much.

Harrer extends a filthy hand. Tsarong warmly takes it.

> TSARONG
> I am Tsarong. Welcome to my home.

EXT. POTALA — DAY

Tsarong waits outside the gates which are heavily protected by two rings of

guards—monk ZINGAGS. After a while, the gates open and the LORD CHAM-
BERLAIN steps out. He is a tall, unyielding man who takes his job as
Emissary to the Dalai Lama very seriously. Tsarong bows to him.

                         TSARONG
     Lord Chamberlain, may I request an audience with the
     Regent and Ministers of the Cabinet. It's about two
     Europeans who've come to Lhasa.

EXT. POTALA STEPS — DAY

Tsarong ascends the long flight of palace steps.

INT. CABINET CHAMBERS — DAY

The REGENT—TATHAG RINPOCHE—sits on a throne only slightly lower
than the one next to him, on which sits the young Dalai Lama. The MINIS-
TERS of the Tibetan Cabinet have convened. And the eight SECRETARIES.
Four Secretaries are laymen. Four are monk officials. Addressing the
Cabinet is a minor secretary—a proud, consummately clever man who
comports himself with the grandeur of an aristocrat. He is NGAWANG
JIGME. Unlike the Ministers in their brocade finery, Ngawang wears a sim-
ple brown robe. He holds a letter in his hand.

                         REGENT
                        (to Ngawang)
     Thank you for reading our letter to the Chinese Mission,
     Ngawang Jigme.
                        (to Ministers)
     What is your opinion? Do you feel it is sufficiently threat-
     ening without insulting their government?

The Ministers murmur and nod. But no one ventures an opinion. With
complete self-possession, Ngawang Jigme bows.

NGAWANG

With respect, Rinpoche, if your intention is to stop the
Chinese from recruiting political allies, demanding they
stop trying to bribe monks is not the most efficient tactic.

(pauses)

The people you should be speaking to are the abbots of the
monasteries in question. They must be warned that, under
no circumstances, should they accept so-called donations
made by the Chinese.

The Regent scowls with displeasure, waves his hand to stop Ngawang.

REGENT

I asked the opinion of the Ministers, Ngawang Jigme, not
the opinion of a mere secretary.

NGAWANG

Forgive me.

He stands there supremely composed, doesn't betray an emotion.

REGENT

You may go now. Start translating the letter. As written.

INT. HALLWAY OF POTALA — DAY

Exiting the Cabinet Chambers, Ngawang nods calmly to Tsarong being
ushered inside. Alone, Ngawang's implacable composure vanishes; deeply
disturbed by the Regent's rebuke, he touches a trembling hand to his
flushed cheek. Hearing VOICES inside the chamber, he gathers his pride,
slowly moves closer to the door. Pries it open a crack and listens.

INT. CABINET CHAMBERS — DAY

Tsarong faces the Dalai Lama, Regent, and Ministers of the Kashag. The
Dalai Lama is transfixed by Tsarong's news.

TSARONG

—Rinpoche, do you realize how many men could survive such an ordeal?

(shakes his head)

They deserve our respect. If we return them to India, surely they'll go back to prison.

REGENT

(unimpressed)

They have no purpose here, no place to live.

TSARONG

I have invited them to stay in my guest quarters.

Assuming you grant them permission to remain in Lhasa, of course.

REGENT

Invite them to live in your home? Why?

TSARONG

Must one have a reason to help those in need?

The Dalai Lama looks all around the room to gauge the Ministers' reactions. His roving eye spots Ngawang hidden behind the doorway. The boy smiles in greeting.

Ngawang recoils, mortified that he has been discovered. He quickly closes the doors and hurries down the hallway.

INT. TSARONG GUEST QUARTERS — DAY

Harrer, at a desk, is writing. Scattered on the desk are piles of letters addressed to his son. Aufschnaiter thumbs through a pile of old *Life* magazines, glancing at photos of the war in Europe. The door is abruptly opened and Tashi steps in, sneering lasciviously.

TASHI

Mister Heinrig, Mister Peter, you are having a visitor.

As she walks out, she mutters under her breath...

TASHI

Filthy dogs.

A moment later, a smooth, burnished beauty enters the room—PEMA LHAKI. She has the bones of a model and the brains of a schoolteacher. Sets a wicker basket on a table and faces the men.

PEMA

You do not need to introduce yourselves. I know who you are.
(coolly)

I am Pema Lhaki.

Both men rise to their feet, speechless.

BOTH MEN

Oh.

PEMA

Ngawang Jigme wishes to make a gift to you. So please
take off your clothes.

Astounded, they stand there like timid schoolboys.

PEMA

Come...let's get started. I don't have all day.

They don't quite know what to make of this, but begin to like it.

AUFSCHNAITER

Well...this is extremely nice of Ngawang Jigme.

HARRER

Yes. Extremely. Who is he to be so kind?

She removes a catalogue and a tape measure from her wicker basket; sizes
them up while approaching them.

PEMA

Secretary to the Ministers of the government. He wished to
make you a gift. Of new clothes.
(holds open the catalogue)
Please select your preferred article of clothing.

She hands them the catalogue. It is from Harrod's—the British department
store, located in Calcutta.

CLOSE ON PAGES OF CATALOGUE: Raj dandies pose woodenly in Western suits and ties.

HARRER peers at the catalogue in confusion, then at Pema.

> HARRER
>
> You're a seamstress?

> PEMA
> *(with great dignity)*
>
> I am a tailor, sir.
>
> *(looser)*
>
> The only tailor in Lhasa who has been to Calcutta and can reproduce these silly costumes.

As she holds out the catalogue for him, he can hardly take his eyes off her, struck by her beauty and his close proximity to it.

> HARRER
> *(tries to sound breezy, points to catalogue)*
>
> I'll take this "handsome" tweed jacket and this pair of "sporting" woolen trousers.

Pema nods, turns to Aufschnaiter. Having seen Harrer's obvious interest in her, Aufschnaiter has quietly backed off.

> AUFSCHNAITER
>
> I'll have the same thing, please.

Pema gestures for Harrer to remove his robe. He does, stands bare-chested, in boxer shorts, slightly titillated as she starts to measure his back. He turns to look at her, wants to say something but is tongue-tied.

> PEMA
>
> Please stand still.

She runs the measuring tape down his back and he flinches at her touch.

                              PEMA
Don't move. Please.

                             HARRER
    Sorry.

She begins to measure his chest. Aufschnaiter rolls his eyes when Harrer
takes a deep breath, puffs out his pecs. It has no effect on Pema.

Aufschnaiter smiles to himself, pleased to discover he might have a chance,
after all.

INT. ROOM IN CHINESE MISSION — DAY

Hanging from the walls of a reception room are pictures of SUN YAT-SEN
and CHIANG KAI-SHEK. Ngawang Jigme bows deeply as he is presented to
the AMBAN of the Chinese Mission. The Amban is a sly old lizard with
impeccable manners. Other CHINESE DIPLOMATS are assembled in the room.
All eyes watch as the Amban holds up a letter to Ngawang.

                             AMBAN
    I am told you translated the Cabinet's letter to us,
    Ngawang Jigme.

                            NGAWANG
    Yes, Your Excellency.

                             AMBAN
    Perhaps you can explain. Why do your Ministers demand
    that the Chinese government...
                         (reading letter)
    "Cease making such generous financial contributions to
    Tibet's monasteries"?
                           (pauses)
    Do our gifts displease your government?

                        NGAWANG

I cannot speak for the Regent, nor the Ministers,
Excellence. I am a mere secretary.

                        AMBAN

Not for long, I presume.
                        (smiles)
A man of such obvious talent cannot be satisfied translating
letters. Can he?

Ngawang Jigme stands there calmly, returning the Amban's penetrating
stare.

                        AMBAN

Your diplomatic skills would be richly rewarded here.

                        NGAWANG

Serving my country faithfully is reward enough, Excellence.
                        (pauses)
I ask your permission to take my leave.

The Amban nods and Ngawang Jigme turns toward the door.

EXT. CHINESE MISSION — DAY

Leaving the Mission, Ngawang strains to appear collected, barely glances at
CHINESE WORKERS unloading wooden crates from a yak caravan. As
Ngawang departs, the depth of his agitation at what just transpired
becomes visible. A Chinese worker carting crates into the Mission's side
door waits until Ngawang has disappeared before prying open a box; he
uses a crowbar to wrench off the lid. Removes wadded paper on top. Under
the paper are shipments of GUNS and AMMUNITION.

CAMERA MOVES to the Mission's roof, where more workers build what looks
like a shiny metal Erector Set tower. It is an antenna.

EXT. ROAD NEAR CHINESE MISSION — DAY

Ngawang is advancing up the road, still deeply unsettled. Looking ahead, he sees Harrer and Aufschnaiter a distance away, coming toward him. They are wearing their new suits. In an instant, Ngawang changes his comportment: bears himself with regal poise. When Harrer and Aufschnaiter reach him, Ngawang bows, assuming they have come to pay respects.

                    NGAWANG
        Gentlemen.

Harrer and Aufschnaiter look at each other in confusion.

                    AUFSCHNAITER
        I'm sorry, have we met?

                    NGAWANG
                (a momentary deflation)
        No, we have not. I am Ngawang Jigme.

Both Harrer and Aufschnaiter gasp with embarrassment, bow deeply to Ngawang, who brightens visibly at the show of respect.

                    AUFSCHNAITER
        Forgive us, Ngawang Jigme. And thank you for your
        generous gift.

EXT. TSARONG'S GARDEN — DAY

On a bright, unseasonably warm winter's day, Harrer's putting on a performance for Pema. With tremendous ease and confidence, Harrer has rope tied to his waist, is rappelling down the side of Tsarong's house. Aufschnaiter stiffly observes Harrer ply his charm, while Pema watches Harrer with amused detachment.

                    PEMA
        Still, walking up mountains is a fool's pleasure, Heinrich.

Reaching the ground, a grinning Harrer unties the rope around his waist, retrieves his diary from a nearby table. Opens it and hands it to Pema.

                    HARRER
     Not so foolish, really.

CLOSE ON DIARY: All the newspaper clippings of Harrer's mountaineering triumphs. The awards, medals, citations. Pema politely takes the diary and looks at the clippings.

                    PEMA
     Then this is another great difference between our civiliza-
     tion and yours.
                    (gazes at Harrer)
     You admire the man who pushes his way to the top in any
     walk of life … while we admire the man who abandons his ego.
                    (returns diary)
     The average Tibetan wouldn't think to thrust himself for-
     ward in this way.

Harrer flushes, for once unable to respond.

EXT. STREET IN LHASA — DAY

As snow cascades on Lhasa, Harrer hurries up a street, yanking on his jacket pocket, ripping it off. He heads straight for a shop on a corner.

INT. SHOP — DAY

It is a tailor's shop. Entering, Harrer smiles when he sees Pema crouched down, mending a rip in a MAN'S pants. The man's back is to us; he turns and Harrer is stunned to discover it's Aufschnaiter. Taking a moment to recover, Harrer makes a great show of appearing amused by this serendipity. Holds up his ripped pocket, laughing.

                    HARRER
     Looks like we both need a good tailor today.

Aufschnaiter chokes out a feeble laugh, becomes extremely stilted, unable to speak. Pema's the only one who remains natural, smiles warmly and gestures for Harrer to sit.

EXT. BARKHOR — DAY

As Aufschnaiter lingers behind to let Harrer take center stage with Pema, the three of them meander through the Barkhor—a surreal carnival of the sacred and profane, the center of Lhasa's social life. A row of shops and stalls, gambling parlors, and *chang* (beer) houses line the route around Lhasa's holiest temple, the Jokhang. The route is teeming with merchants, monks, pilgrims, Khampas. Pausing by a stall selling used goods from the West, Pema finds a pair of rusty ice skates.

She stares quizzically at them, speaks quickly in Tibetan to the VENDOR. Aufschnaiter self-consciously steps back to let Harrer move next to Pema.

> HARRER
> Do you like them? I'll buy them for you.

He flashes a dazzling smile. She smiles tactfully in return.

> PEMA
> Thank you, but I don't eat much meat.

Now it's the men's turn to be confused.

> HARRER
> What?

> PEMA
> (points to VENDOR)
> He says they're knives from the West.
> (the VENDOR nods)
> You put them on your feet, to cut meat.

Harrer and Aufschnaiter laugh loudly. Watching them, Pema starts laughing, too. Seeing her solemn face break open in a wide smile is such a lovely sight. Aufschnaiter picks up a pair of skates.

> AUFSCHNAITER
>
> They're ice skates.

Baffled, Pema looks first at Aufschnaiter, then Harrer.

> HARRER
>
> You put them on your feet, but then you glide... sort of dance on ice.

> PEMA
>
> Why?

> AUFSCHNAITER
> *(gently)*
>
> It's just another fool's pleasure, Pema.

Turning back to lock eyes with Aufschnaiter, Pema sees the depth of his anguish at continually stepping back for Harrer. Aufschnaiter is in love with Pema. And she knows it.

EXT. FROZEN LAKE BELOW POTALA — DAY

A few people hover inquisitively near the frozen lake as Harrer, Aufschnaiter, and Pema step gingerly out to the bright glazed ice wearing skates.

ON THE ICE: Pema wobbles, and the two men quickly offer their arms for support. She takes both men's. With arms linked, the three of them skate a few feet together. Then Pema falls. Acting first, Harrer extends his hand to help her up. Brushing herself off, Pema waits until Aufschnaiter has extended his hand. She calmly takes Aufschnaiter's hand and lets him pull her to her feet while Harrer stands by, bewildered.

EXT. LAKE — LATER

A large crowd of monks and lay people has gathered to watch them. A YOUNG MONK puts on a pair of skates; curious Tibetans surround him. He hobbles out to the ice and promptly falls on his ass.

ON THE ICE: Now it's Harrer who lingers behind, unsure of himself as Aufschnaiter patiently teaches Pema how to balance, kick, and glide. The two of them skate together in a small circle, never taking their eyes off each other—a quiet, steady happiness. As Harrer watches on the periphery, he seems bewildered by Pema's obvious preference for Aufschnaiter, and heart-broken by the loss of his hopes. Realizing his chance is over, he makes an atypically gracious gesture. He backs away, leaving them alone. While Pema and Aufschnaiter skate around him, Harrer spots the monk teetering onto the ice. Makes his way over to him. Gently takes the monk's hand and leads him out to the center.

POV — THROUGH TELESCOPE LENS:

Follow the lens as it moves with Harrer holding the monk's hand, gliding him across the lake and teaching him how to skate.

EXT. ROOF OF POTALA — DAY

The Dalai Lama is mesmerized as he watches the ice skating through his telescope.

INT. TSARONG'S GUEST HOUSE — DAY

Harrer at a desk writes a letter to his son.

> HARRER (V.O.)
> I try to picture you, Rolf, and this is what I see: a young boy who is stong . . . and brave. A boy who isn't afraid . . .

148

He pauses, lost for a moment. Stares out the window.

> HARRER (V.O.)
> To learn from his mistakes.

EXT. HOUSE IN COUNTRY — LATE DAY

Harrer canters up a dirt path and tethers his horse outside a lovely, isolated house. After a moment, Aufschnaiter and Pema come out to greet him; she wears a striped *chuba* over her apron. CLOSE ON THEIR HANDS twined together—both wear wedding rings. Pema steps forward, reaching out to take Harrer's hand in greeting. Straining to appear light-hearted, he points to her wedding ring.

> HARRER
> Hello, married woman.

> PEMA
> Hello, bachelor man.

Then he and Aufschnaiter awkwardly embrace.

INT. AUFSCHNAITER AND PEMA'S HOUSE — NIGHT

Harrer sits across from Pema as a young MANSERVANT serves them dinner. Aufschnaiter hovers by the radio, listening to a BBC news broadcast.

> RADIO NEWSCASTER (V.O.)
> The Japanese Army is facing a growing challenge, not from China's Unified Front, but from the powerful Chinese Communist Army . . . Under the control of Mao Tse-tung, the Eighth Route and New Fourth Armies total nearly half a million men and women . . .

Aufschnaiter turns down the volume, takes a seat at the table.

AUFSCHNAITER

Rumor is the Communists have taken control of most of
northern and eastern China.

HARRER
(nods)

Rumor? It's a fact, Peter. They'll beat the Japanese, then start
a civil war. Ngawang Jigme keeps me up to date on China's
war news.

The manservant leaves them to their dinner. Before eating, Pema and
Aufschnaiter fold their hands in prayer and murmur a chant. Harrer notices
Aufschnaiter and Pema are both wearing red strings—protection cords—
around their necks. This makes him feel even more an outsider than he
already does. After the prayer, Aufschnaiter digs into his food.

AUFSCHNAITER

So, how are things at Kungo Tsarong's?

HARRER

I have no idea. I moved out five months ago.

AUFSCHNAITER
(taken aback)

It's been that long since we've seen you?

HARRER

Yes. Apparently it has.

There is an awkward silence.

PEMA

And have you been busy?

HARRER

Oh yes, you see, I'm on the government payroll. They've

hired me to survey the entire city of Lhasa. Of course, your place is too far away to be included on my map.

> PEMA

We like our privacy.

> HARRER

Yes. I've noticed.

Aufschnaiter gives Harrer an empathetic smile; making Harrer even more brittle. Pema doesn't seem to notice how rude Harrer is being.

> PEMA

What about women? Have you met anyone you like?

> HARRER
> (laughs tightly)

Since I failed miserably with an Austrian wife, leaping into an exotic failure with a Tibetan wife seems a bit misguided.
> (sharply)

But to answer your question, no. I haven't.

Pema lifts her head and locks eyes with Harrer, disarming him with her simplicity and kindness.

> PEMA

A friend's good fortune is a blessing, Heinrich. I'm sorry you resent ours.

Harrer has to avert his eyes from Pema's sympathetic gaze.

> PEMA

You must be very lonely and sad.

EXT. STREET IN LHASA — DAY

Harrer drags a surveyor's theodolite down a street, sets it upright, listlessly

jots down a few notes on a map, then peers into the device. POV—
THROUGH CROSS HAIRS OF THEODOLITE: Ngawang Jigme strides up the
street. When he's only a foot away from the lens, he leans down and speaks
to Harrer.

NGAWANG

Heinrich. The war is over.

HARRER
(*dutiful response*)

Have the Communists won?

NGAWANG

Your war, my friend. Germany has surrendered.

Harrer jerks his head up, speechless. It takes a few moments to register the full impact of the news. He just walks away, leaving the theodolite and everything else behind.

NGAWANG
(stunned)

Where are you going?

HARRER

Home. To Austria.

INT. HARRER'S HOUSE — EVENING

With newfound energy, Harrer's gathering his few possessions, packing his bags when he hears a LIGHT TAPPING on the door. He opens the door. Like an alley cat, Tashi pads inside, presenting a letter.

TASHI

Letter for you.
(plaintive)
We miss you.

CLOSE ON LETTER: It is from Austria. A child's handwritten scrawl has addressed the letter to MR. HEINRICH HARRER, at Tsarong's house.

HARRER takes the letter, ecstatic. Kisses Tashi's forehead.

HARRER

I miss you, too.

INT. DESK AT HARRER'S HOUSE — LATER

Harrer rips open the envelope, reads the letter. And deflates. In a hollow whisper, he reads it aloud.

> HARRER
>
> "Dear Mister Heinrich Harrer, You are not my father. Please stop writing me letters. Rolf Immendorf."

INT. HOUSE — NIGHT

Harrer lies in bed, sleepless. He rises, grabs his blanket, and heads outside.

EXT. HOUSE — MORNING

Harrer crashed in a stupor outside his house. He lifts his head at the sound of HORSE HOOVES pounding the road. An agile MESSENGER stops and leaps from the horse, bowing like Jiminy Cricket.

> MESSENGER
>
> Honorable Heinrich Harrer—a letter for you.

He gravely presents the letter. Harrer shakes his head.

> HARRER
>
> Honorable Heinrich Harrer doesn't want any more letters.

The messenger places the letter on Harrer's chest.

> MESSENGER
>
> With respect, sir. It is from the Great Mother of His Holiness the Dalai Lama.

EXT. GATES OF DALAI LAMA'S MOTHER'S RESIDENCE — DAY

Following the messenger, Harrer is ushered through massive, ornamental gates.

EXT. COURTYARD OF DALAI LAMA'S MOTHER'S RESIDENCE — DAY

A ceremonial canopy has been erected at one end of a sweeping courtyard artfully landscaped with gardens and fountains. Under the canopy is a throne. And seated on the throne is the Dalai Lama's mother. Proffering a white *khata*, Harrer slowly approaches her. With an air of quiet intelligence, she studies him. Reaching her, Harrer bows and presents the *khata*.

MOTHER
(accepting the khata)
Thank you for coming, Mister Harrer.

HARRER
Thank you for inviting me, Great Mother.

She gestures to a chair placed in front of her throne. Harrer takes a seat. They cautiously appraise one another.

MOTHER
Do you know the rules of protocol concerning my son?

HARRER
(confused)
No, not exactly. I know one bows and performs prostrations. Why?

MOTHER
(doesn't answer the question)
When you are in the presence of His Holiness, you must be standing, bent in obeisance, hands folded in supplication. If seated, you must always be seated lower than he. Never look him in the eye. Do not speak before he does. Always refer to him as "Your Holiness." Never turn your back to him. And never, never touch him.
(pauses)
He is the reincarnation of Avalokiteshvara, the Bodhisattva of Compassion.

HARRER
That's a lot of protocol.

(gets no response)
Just out of curiosity, does His Holiness have a proper name?

MOTHER

His name at birth was Lhamo Dondrub. But after his recognition, he was renamed Jetsun Jamphel Ngawang Lobsang Yeshi Tenzin Gyatso—Holy Lord, Gentle Glory, Eloquent, Compassionate, Learned Defender of the Faith, Ocean of Wisdom.

HARRER

That is a lot of names.

She can't tell whether he's being sarcastic or not. Somberly folds her hands and studies him, making him uncomfortable.

MOTHER

His Holiness the Dalai Lama would like to meet you, Mister Harrer.

Harrer can hardly believe what he has just heard.

MOTHER

Since his advisors have not permitted a private audience with you, His Holiness has asked me to bring you along to my monthly audience.

HARRER

I am extremely honored and moved.

MOTHER

As you should be.

EXT. GATES OF POTALA — DAY

Harrer nervously approaches the heavily fortified gates, remaining a few paces behind the Dalai Lama's mother. Without hesitation, the gates are swiftly opened and the flanks of Zingags and bodyguards bow in reverence to the Great Mother.

EXT. POTALA STEPS — DAY

Harrer and the Great Mother ascend a long flight of steps.

INT. CORRIDOR OF POTALA — DAY

Led by the monks, Harrer and the Great Mother are whisked quickly down dark, labyrinthine corridors—lit only by the dull glow of butter lamps. A monk opens a door and soft light floods inside.

INT. RECEPTION HALL — DAY

They enter a vast hall filled with *thangkas* depicting the pantheon of Buddhas and Bodhisattvas. Prominently displayed in the center is a jewel-studded, delicately composed image of serenity: a statue of Avalokiteshvara, the thousand-armed Bodhisattva of Compassion. A monk leads them toward the Dalai Lama's official reception room. The Dalai Lama's mother gives Harrer an expensive silk *khata*. He nervously holds it in both hands, afraid to drop it. The doors open, and they are ushered inside.

INT. RECEPTION ROOM — DAY

Entering first, Harrer takes a few steps and involuntarily looks up to the Dalai Lama's high throne. He is shocked to see the thirteen-year-old avatar grinning excitedly at him, like a long-lost friend. A look of surprise and deep, overwhelming pleasure lights Harrer's face. The two of them lock eyes, staring. Utterly scandalized, the Dalai Lama's mother bows and prostrates. Harrer dutifully bows. Tries a clunky prostration and nearly trips. The Dalai Lama laughs with delight.

Aware of the mother's censorious gaze, Harrer approaches the throne, head lowered. Extends his arms to present the *khata*. He doesn't know what to say.

HARRER

Hello.

Smiling, the Dalai Lama takes the *khata*. Then does something strange. He leans over the edge of the throne, peers in wonder at Harrer's blond hair. Gently tugs on the hair. Rumples it with both hands, musses it up.

DALAI LAMA

Yellow head.
(*points to an arm*)
You have hair on your arms, too? And legs?

Harrer eagerly pulls up his sleeve to show the Dalai Lama. Then lifts his pant leg.

HARRER

Let's see yours.

MOTHER

Mister Harrer.

HARRER
(*turns*)
Yes, Great Mother?

She sternly shakes her head. As if pulled away from an enchanted dream, Harrer turns back to the Dalai Lama and bows.

HARRER

Your Holiness, it is a great honor to meet you.

He heads back to his seat. Remembers he's not to turn his back to the Dalai Lama and awkwardly attempts walking backwards. He takes his seat and politely waits for the Dalai Lama to speak first.

Continued on page 163

158

IMAGES FROM THE MAKING OF
SEVEN YEARS IN TIBET

~

The color photographs that follow were shot on location in the Argentine Andes and British Columbia, Canada, by David Appleby, Pat Morrow, and Bill Kaye. They document the meticulous detail with which the *Seven Years in Tibet* production team re-created the Tibet of Heinrich Harrer's era, as well as some of the film's memorable characters and dramatic moments. Captions are found on pages 161–162.

CAPTIONS FOR COLOR PHOTOGRAPHS FROM
SEVEN YEARS IN TIBET

1. The young Dalai Lama, played by eight-year-old Sonam Wangchuk, is escorted on a procession through Lhasa.

2. Heinrich Harrer, played by Brad Pitt, meets Peter Aufschnaiter, leader of the Nanga Parbat expedition (David Thewlis) at the train station in Graz, Austria.

3. Base camp on "Nanga Parbat," as the crew prepares a location shot in the Coast Range of British Columbia.

4. Heinrich Harrer (Pitt) climbs on Nanga Parbat. Brad Pitt and David Thewlis received a crash course in mountaineering from Austrian experts.

5. Members of the Nanga Parbat team struggle up a slope. The terrain and conditions in British Columbia were very similar to the Himalaya.

6. The young Dalai Lama (Sonam Wangchuk) descends into the courtyard of the Potala during a procession.

7. The young Dalai Lama (Sonam Wangchuk) peers out through the curtains of his palanquin at a world that cannot look him in the eye.

8. Jetsun Pema, sister of His Holiness, portrays their mother, the revered Great Mother, in the film.

9. Filming the procession; director Annaud stands on the dolly at right.

10. David Thewlis as Peter Aufschnaiter, bargaining for food at a Tibetan bazaar.

11. Aufschnaiter (Thewlis) and Harrer (Pitt) during the period when they are reduced to wandering beggars in the Tibetan countryside.

12. Pilgrims entering the western gate of Lhasa, the "Forbidden City."

13. The Japanese actor Mako as the generous Tibetan nobleman Tsarong, who befriends the German refugees.

14. Pema Dorjee, the Lhasa tailor who marries Aufschnaiter, is played by Lhakpa Tsamchoe, a striking and scholarly young woman who works for the Tibetan Youth Congress.

15. Pilgrims gather outside the film's re-creation of Lhasa's famed Jokhang temple.

16. A curious Dalai Lama (here played by fourteen-year-old Jamyang Wangchuk) at his first encounter with the "yellow head" Harrer.

17. Brad Pitt, as Harrer, rejoices at the completion of the movie theater he has built for the Dalai Lama.

18. Tibetan monks—who portray themselves in the film—in front of a butter sculpture, a traditional art form that symbolizes the fleeting nature of existence.

19. Ngawang Jigme, played by B. D. Wong, crosses the makeshift airstrip outside Lhasa to greet the arriving Chinese generals.

20. As the Chinese generals enter the Jokhang, they are about to walk through and desecrate a sand *mandala* painstakingly created by monks.

21. The Dalai Lama (Jamyang) addresses the Chinese generals.

22. In this scene, Tibetan leaders are forced to sign a surrender agreement with the invading Chinese.

23. B. D. Wong as Ngawang looks out of the window of the Chinese mission in Lhasa.

24. The Chinese generals enter the Jokhang.

25. Harrer (Pitt) and the Dalai Lama (Jamyang) bid farewell to each other on the roof of the Potala.

26. Harrer (Pitt) receives his first and last blessing from his young friend.

27. Harrer (Pitt) walks through Lhasa's Western Gate.

With urgent seriousness, the Dalai Lama begins the audience.

                    DALAI LAMA

Do you like movies?

                    HARRER

Well...I haven't seen one in about eight years. But as I recall, yes, I do.

                    DALAI LAMA

So do I.

                    HARRER

I'm glad to know that, Your Holiness.

                    DALAI LAMA

I have a movie projector. And films. One of female dancers being hatched out of eggs.

                    HARRER

That could be a bit racy.
                    (the mother clears her throat)
It sounds wonderfully educational, Your Holiness.

                    DALAI LAMA

I want to build a movie house. Here at the Potala. With seats and everything.

                    HARRER

Seats would be advisable.

                    DALAI LAMA

Can you build it?

                    HARRER

Excuse me?

DALAI LAMA

Can you build a movie house for me? My advisors cannot disapprove and you will be well paid.

The mother knits her eyebrows in consternation. She wasn't informed of this plan. Now the Dalai Lama speaks in a fast torrent of words, desperate to say everything at once.

DALAI LAMA

And you will have to come here every day to build it. Every single day. And when you're here, you will visit me. We can have conversations. On many topics. I would like to learn about the world you come from.
(breathless)
For example...where is Paris, France? And what is a Molotov Cocktail? And who is Jack the Ripper?

MOTHER

Kundun...

Realizing she has interrupted her son, she stops herself. The Dalai Lama knows he's going out on a limb, but is determined to have his way.

DALAI LAMA

You can tell me many things.

Harrer folds his hands together, bows his head. Then glances surreptitiously at the Dalai Lama, full of admiration.

HARRER

I am proud to be of service, Your Holiness.

EXT. FIELD NEAR LAKE — DAY

A shovel stabs the ground—clots of dirt are flung off it. In a construction site beside the lake in back of the Potala, Harrer and twenty Tibetan

COOLIES work up a sweat clearing ground for the movie theater. Each pitchful of dirt causes a deeper sense of unrest among the coolies. Finally, they drop to their knees, crying in agony.

COOLIES

Worms!

Harrer watches uncomprehendingly as the sobbing coolies gently pluck the worms from their spades and place them in safe spots on the ground. The foreman—a soft spoken young man with a long, sensitive face—TENZIN—searches the dirt for more.

TENZIN

No more disturbing worms.

He lovingly sets another worm on the ground, peering up at Harrer's admonishing figure.

> TENZIN
>
> In a past life, this innocent creature could have been your mother.

INT. DALAI LAMA'S RECEPTION ROOM — DAY

The Dalai Lama sits on his throne, laughing loudly at Harrer's incredulous recounting of the worm incident.

> DALAI LAMA
>
> —But you see, Tibetans believe all living creatures were their mothers in a past life. So we must show them respect and repay their kindness.
>
> *(becoming serious)*
>
> And never, never harm anything that lives. You can't ask devout people to disregard a precious teaching.

> HARRER
>
> But Your Holiness, with all due respect, you want the theater finished in this lifetime, don't you? We don't have time to rescue every worm in the ground.

> DALAI LAMA
>
> You have a clever mind. Think of a solution. And in the meantime, you can explain to me—what is an elevator?

EXT. FIELD NEAR LAKE — DAY

A solution to the worm problem has been devised: As coolies work on construction of the movie theater, cadres of CHANTING MONKS carefully transport all endangered insects and worms to safe havens in another area, allowing the coolies to work without interruption. There is a spirit of high cheerfulness to the proceedings.

INT. ROOM — DAY

CLOSE ON A HUGE HAND-DRAWN MAP OF THE WORLD. With drawings of vegetation, wildlife, terrain in each country. A HAND holding a crayon pauses over Antarctica.

> DALAI LAMA (O.S.)
> What kind of animals live in Antarctica?

EXT. GLASS APARTMENT ON ROOF OF POTALA — DAY

Through the glass of a small apartment on the roof, see the Dalai Lama and Harrer hunched over the map, which takes up the whole floor of the room.

> HARRER
> Very cold animals.

INT. ATTIC STOREROOM IN POTALA — DAY

In a room brimming with expensive gifts, a rusty Austin-Healy has been placed on bricks. Harrer in the passenger seat teaches the Dalai Lama to drive; how to use the stick shift, turn signal, rear view mirror. As the Dalai Lama gleefully spins the steering wheel, Harrer covers his face with his hands and the two of them scream in mock terror.

EXT. BANKS OF RIVER KYICHU — DAY

The sky swirls with hundreds of exotic, brilliantly colored kites. On the field by the river, Tibetan children and adults indulge in a national pastime: kite flying and picnicking.

The field is dotted with tents—many of them are huge with elaborate appliqué symbols on the sides.

Monks, nobles, and commoners freely mingle together, eating and playing in the sun. By the river, MUSICIANS play traditional Tibetan folk music, some are step dancing. A HORN SOUNDS and the fun and games abruptly end. The crowd stands stiffly at attention, watching the Regent and Ministers of the Cabinet float up the river in coracles, shielded from the sun by servants holding large parasols. The people on the banks bow as the Regent steps out of his coracle and is led to the largest tent on the field.

INT. TENT — DAY

Outside a lavishly ornamented tent, Ngawang Jigme hosts a luncheon. In place of his drab brown robe, Ngawang now wears stately brocade robes. Among the guests—Tsarong, Pema, Aufschnaiter, Harrer, and two monks. At the head of the table, Ngawang is talking to Aufschnaiter.

> AUFSCHNAITER
> *(teasing, re Ngawang's new silk robes)*
> The robe of a Minister is much finer than your old brown robe, isn't it?
> *(smiles)*
> You must be very clever to get such a good promotion.

Ngawang offers one of his cryptic, evasive smiles.

> NGAWANG
> I did not intend to be a secretary forever.

INT. HARRER'S BEDROOM NIGHT

Waking with a start, Harrer bolts upright, hears CLAPPING and HISSING outside his window. He creeps out of bed to his doorway, peers outside.

EXT. STREET NIGHT

A group of agitated TOWNSPEOPLE point up to the sky, clapping and hissing. A HAGGARD WOMAN sees Harrer and mutters forlornly.

HAGGARD WOMAN
Evil omen... evil omen...

Harrer looks up at the sky.

POV SKY

Hanging from the heavens is a bright HORSE-TAILED COMET.

INT. TSARONG'S STUDY — DAY

Through the window, see Tashi and other servants in the garden, pointing upward. Even in daylight, the comet still blazes, suspended in the clear blue sky. Tsarong sits at his desk, looking pale and stricken as he listens to the NEWS on the radio.

RADIO ANNOUNCER (V.O.)
...From his headquarters in Peking, Chairman Mao Tse-tung was triumphantly proclaimed leader of the new People's Republic of China...

INT. AUFSCHNAITER'S HOUSE — DAY

As Pema stands in the doorway, staring up at the comet, Aufschnaiter listens to the NEWS on his radio.

RADIO ANNOUNCER (V.O.)
...Chairman Mao vowed the first task of the Communist regime is to reunite the Chinese motherland.

EXT. HARRER'S PORCH — DAY

Working with quiet concentration, Harrer pots geraniums in tin cans, does not react to the news heard drifting from the radio inside his house.

RADIO ANNOUNCER (V.O.)
He declared that the remote kingdom of Tibet is an integral part of Chinese territory...

INT. CABINET CHAMBERS — DAY

An emergency session of the Cabinet has been convened. WE MOVE across the faces of the Ministers of the Cabinet as they listen to an ATTENDANT read the rest of the broadcast aloud. Come to rest on Ngawang Jigme, dressed in opulent brocade, just like all the other Ministers.

                    ATTENDANT
        . . . "And must join the great new Republic."

The Regent bellows from his throne.

                    REGENT
        The People's Republic of China is advised: The government
        of Tibet recognizes no foreign sovereign. We are an inde-
        pendent nation.
                (peering at all the Ministers)
        They are further advised that all Chinese officials will be
        expelled from our borders.

All the ministers nod their approval. Except one: Ngawang Jigme. When the Regent peers down at him, Ngawang holds a steady, provocative gaze, refusing to communicate his approval to his superior.

EXT. CHINESE MISSION — DAY

Near the Mission, a band plays. Tea is served under a canopy. An aggrieved, sullen assembly of DIPLOMATS, other CHINESE AGENTS remains unmoved by the lavish presentation of traditional Tibetan farewell courtesies. The other Ministers of the Cabinet mechanically perform their tasks, but Ngawang takes pains to appear conciliatory. Moving down the line he offers the diplomats *khatas*, gently murmuring:

                    NGAWANG
        May you have happiness and prosperity.

Reaching the Amban, Ngawang offers a *khata*. As he wraps the scarf around the Amban's neck, he also murmurs:

NGAWANG

May you have happiness and prosperity.

The Amban nods and takes Ngawang's hand. Turns it over and examines the palm. Traces a line across a crease.

AMBAN

You have a long life line, Ngawang Jigme. Unlike others here.

Ngawang jerks his hand away.

EXT. MISSION — LATER

Ngawang stands alone outside the Mission, watching workers remove the Chinese flag and board up the premises. On the roof, the antenna stands tall, construction completed. Then Ngawang stares at his cold, trembling palm, wipes it on his sleeve and walks away.

EXT. CONSTRUCTION SITE — DAY

Harrer hard at work with the construction crew; the theater is half-finished.

INT. ROOM IN POTALA — DAY

In a room overlooking the construction site, the Dalai Lama chants prayers with his tutors, their voices rise and fall in steady, hypnotic rhythms. While chanting, the Dalai Lama glances through the open window at Harrer working on the theater down below, smiles to himself. Trijang Rinpoche quietly rises, closes the window's shutters.

EXT. BESIDE A RIVER — DAY

A small throne lies empty on an expensive Chinese carpet. The Dalai Lama sits cross-legged beside Harrer, who rotates a globe in front of a butter lamp. Light glows on one side of the globe.

> HARRER
>
> —When you face the light, it's day. When you're in shadow, it's night. So when the sun in rising in Lhasa, it's setting far to the west, in New York City, for example. That's why it's not the same time everywhere.
>
> *(solicitously)*
>
> Does that answer your question?

Nodding, the Dalai Lama spots the poker-faced Master of the Kitchen approaching and he quickly hops onto his throne. Both are silent as the Master serves the Dalai Lama butter tea, covering his mouth with a hand so as not to breathe on the serving. Taking his leave, he walks backwards. The moment he's gone, the Dalai Lama scrambles off the throne, impulsively takes Harrer's hand in his.

> DALAI LAMA
>
> Tell me more, tell me more.

Holding the boy's hand in his, Harrer basks in happiness.

> HARRER
>
> What do you want to know?

INT. ATTIC STOREROOM IN POTALA — DAY

In a dark hidden corner, Harrer sets up a radio while the Dalai Lama holds a flashlight for him to see. Harrer attaches wires from a large portable battery to the back of radio.

> HARRER
>
> In a few minutes, you'll be entering the world of mass media, Your Holiness.

DALAI LAMA

I can hear news from all over the planet?

HARRER

I don't know if they have live broadcasts from the Tonga
Islands, but generally speaking, yeah.

DALAI LAMA

Do you listen to news from your country?

HARRER
(busy working on radio)
Austria? Not very often. Give me some light over here.

He points and the Dalai Lama shines the flashlight on the side of the radio.

DALAI LAMA

Why? It's your home.

HARRER

Not anymore.

DALAI LAMA

But don't you have friends and family there?

The Dalai Lama is so intrigued, he keeps turning to look at Harrer, moving the flashlight.

HARRER

A few friends. No family. Hold the light steady,
Your Holiness.

DALAI LAMA

Why? Is everyone dead?

HARRER
(teasing)
Do you know, there's another sentence construction aside
from the question. You might try it some time.
(goes back to work on the radio)
I was married. But I'm divorced.

DALAI LAMA
What did you do?

Harrer makes a great effort to appear busy with his task, doesn't want the
Dalai Lama to see his face. But he also can't lie to him.

HARRER
I didn't want a child. So I ran away to climb a mountain.

The Dalai Lama is shocked.

DALAI LAMA
You have a child, Heinrig?

HARRER
Though I've never met him.

With great relief, he manages to get the radio working and a loud CRACKLE
OF STATIC bursts through the box. He turns to the Dalai Lama, anxious to
drop the subject.

HARRER
Here. Let me show you how this works.

EXT. CONSTRUCTION SITE — DAY

Long electrical wires drape from the open doorway of the theater to the
rusted Austin Healy, ensconced in a shed next to the theater. Harrer is bent
under the hood of car, clamps chargers to the battery, then shouts.

174

HARRER

Okay. Give it all you've got, Tenzin.

Tenzin inside jeep REVS the engine. Harrer races to the movie theater, following the line of electrical wires.

INT. MOVIE THEATER — DAY

The wires connect to the projector in a glass-enclosed booth. Harrer flicks on a switch and a sharp BEAM OF LIGHT shoots from the projector. The coolies in the doorway race to the beam of light and ecstatically try to grasp it in their hands.

EXT. HARRER'S HOUSE — EVENING

Walking underneath handmade Christmas lights strung outside Harrer's house, a flock of familiar faces makes its way to the front door: Ngawang, Tsarong, Tashi, Pema, Aufschnaiter, the Master of the Kitchen, Tenzin, and the men who worked on the movie theater.

INT. HARRER'S LIVING ROOM — EVENING

Painstaking care has been given to the decorations for a traditional Christmas celebration—a tree lit with candles, boughs of Evergreens, Christmas stockings. And a QUARTET OF MONKS wailing a tone-deaf version of "Silent Night" on oboes and flutes. Harrer at the entrance greets his guests, gives each person a wrapped gift.

HARRER

Happy Christmas.

Astonished and delighted, Aufschnaiter steps forward in the line of guests. Harrer gives him a small wrapped box.

HARRER

Happy Christmas, Peter.

EXT. COURTYARD OUTSIDE HARRER'S HOUSE — NIGHT

Big band music plays, all the Tibetan celebrants swirl around the courtyard doing a bizarre version of swing. The party is raucous, high-spirited.

INT. LIVING ROOM — NIGHT

Aufschnaiter sits alone at an empty table, the remains of a feast spread in front of him. He peers down at the gift in his hands. Unwraps it. Inside the box is a familiar-looking watch. Touched beyond words, Aufschnaiter holds up the watch, peers at the inscription on the back. The inscription reads: TO PETER FROM FATHER. MONT BLANC—MAY 4, 1932. Then, Aufschnaiter reads a card enclosed in box.

CLOSE ON CARD: It reads: "I found it in a shop on the Barkhor. It has traveled a long way and finally come back home. Thank you for your friendship. Heinrich."

EXT. COURTYARD — NIGHT

Aufschnaiter steps out to the porch overlooking the courtyard, sees Harrer down below, and lifts his wrist to show him the watch. While Aufschnaiter comes down the steps, Harrer makes his way through the crowded dance floor. They meet at the bottom of the stairs.

> AUFSCHNAITER
> It is . . . incredible.
> *(pauses, moved)*
> Thank you for saving my life.

The two friends embrace. Just then, someone bumps into the radio, changing the station. And everyone is jolted by the sound of a SHRILL CHINESE VOICE shrieking from the radio.

> CHINESE VOICE
> —The Dalai Lama is a wolf in monk's clothes! Tibet must be liberated from religious oppressors!

A dark silence falls over the crowd. Harrer looks up, calling out.

                    HARRER
    Turn that off—

                CHINESE VOICE (V.O.)
    Tibet must be liberated from foreign imperialists!
    They control Tibet's corrupt government!

                    TSARONG
                 (*steps forward*)
    You and Peter are the only foreigners in our country.

The VOICE on the radio shouts back.

                CHINESE VOICE (V.O.)
    Tibet must be liberated! This is the People's Liberation
    Army's task for the new year! Tibet must be liberated!

EXT. VILLAGE IN TIBET — LATE DAY

People's Liberation Army SOLDIERS drag a crying young MONK and his
elderly LAMA to the center of the street. They force a gun into the monk's
hands, demand that he kill his teacher. Sobbing, the monk throws himself
at his lama's feet. The soldiers kick him.

More SOLDIERS ransack a monastery nearby. Burn sacred scriptures. A rabid
Chinese soldier shoots bullets through a statue of the Buddha, lops off the
head of Avalokiteshvara with a saber.

Back on the street, the bloodied young monk is propped up by more soldiers.
Ramming the gun into his fist, they order him to fire. His lama sits calmly,
holds an enduring, compassionate gaze with his student, silently giving him
permission to shoot. As the hysterical monk raises the gun to fire . . .

INT. DALAI LAMA'S BEDROOM — NIGHT

The Dalai Lama wakes up and cries out.

INT. WAITING ROOM OF DALAI LAMA'S BED CHAMBERS — NIGHT

Harrer is ushered inside by the kindly old Sweeper.

> SWEEPER
> He asked for you, Mister Heinrig.

The Sweeper points to the door leading to the bedroom. Harrer opens it and steps inside.

INT. DALAI LAMA'S BEDROOM — NIGHT

The Dalai Lama sits on the edge of his bed, weeping uncontrollably. Standing awkwardly in front of him, Harrer doesn't know whether he should sit on the Dalai Lama's bed or not.

> DALAI LAMA
> They were destroying the village I was born in—Takster.
> In Amdo. It was terrible.

> HARRER
> You had a bad dream, Kundun. It was just a dream.

> DALAI LAMA
> But it was so real. Where did it come from?

Harrer is at a loss to explain that.

> DALAI LAMA
> My mind could never imagine such terrible things.

Throwing protocol out the window, Harrer sits beside the Dalai Lama and wraps his arm around him.

INT. DALAI LAMA'S WAITING ROOM — NIGHT

Unable to sleep, Harrer stares out at

POV — THROUGH WINDOWS: The snowcapped Himalayas glowing milky white in the darkness.

HARRER hears the DOOR OPEN. Looks up as the Dalai Lama steps into the waiting room and sits down.

> DALAI LAMA
> I can't sleep. I'm afraid the dream will come back.

> HARRER
> We could have an insomniac's slumber party.

> DALAI LAMA
> Tell me a story, Heinrig.

(*looks out at mountains*)
Tell me a story about climbing mountains.

HARRER

That's one way to fall asleep. Those stories bore even me.

DALAI LAMA

Then tell me what you love about it.

Harrer wasn't prepared for that.

HARRER

What do I ...?

He thinks a moment.

HARRER

The absolute simplicity. That's what I love.
(*pauses*)
You have a purpose. Your mind is clear. And calm. Suddenly, the light becomes sharper. Sounds are richer. All you
feel is the deep, powerful presence of life.
(*pauses, embarrassed*)
I've only felt that way one other time before.

DALAI LAMA

When?

Harrer locks eyes with the Dalai Lama.

HARRER

In your presence, Kundun.

INT. GOVERNMENT CHAMBERS OF POTALA — DAY

In the chambers, a mood of subdued hysteria prevails. Tsarong and Harrer
walk briskly through a catacomb of offices, on a mission.

TSARONG

The Chinese have already secured much of the northern border region. They've ransacked a village, destroyed a monastery. Burned scriptures and defaced holy relics. We've been told they've even killed some monks.

Slowing down, Harrer grows faint.

HARRER

Which village?

TSARONG

Takster. In Amdo. It's where His Holiness was born.

Harrer reels backward for a moment, taking this in. Up ahead, Aufschnaiter waits outside the Cabinet Chambers. He greets Tsarong, who turns back and gestures for Harrer to hurry up. In a daze, Harrer follows the two of them into the Chambers.

INT. CABINET CHAMBERS — DAY

The Regent looks deflated, all the fight knocked out of him. He nods dully to Harrer and Aufschnaiter, then turns his attention to Tsarong.

REGENT

Kungo Tsarong, when you were Defense Minister to the previous Dalai Lama...

Harrer goes pale with additional shock—glances over at Aufschnaiter, who clearly didn't know this, either. The Regent senses their surprise.

REGENT

He doesn't boast about his achievements.
(back to Tsarong)
You wanted to reorganize the Army. Can you do it now?
I will appoint you Minister again.

181

TSARONG

The People's Liberation Army is one million troops strong, Rinpoche. We are eight thousand men. With fifty pieces of artillery and a few hundred mortars and machine guns. The task is hopeless.

REGENT

Then you refuse the appointment?

TSARONG

No, Rinpoche. I accept it with honor.

The Regent turns his sad, imploring eyes on Harrer and Aufschnaiter.

REGENT

You two know about wars. What type of weapons do you recommend?

Harrer and Aufschnaiter don't know whether to laugh or cry at the desperate absurdity of the question.

EXT. COURTYARD OF POTALA — DAY

Hurrying down the main staircase, Harrer steps into the Potala's principal courtyard and encounters a scene of chaos and confusion. Frantic people are dragging crates of weapons and ammunition into the Potala, nervous Ministers are huddled in a group, watching. Ngawang is among them. The whole group turns as Harrer rushes toward them.

HARRER

What's happening?

NGAWANG

We've heard Chinese troops are advancing toward our northern borders.

HARRER
(*heartsick*)
Where is His Holiness?

Ngawang points to the movie theater on field down below.

INT. MOVIE THEATER — DAY

Sitting alone in the theater, the Dalai Lama watches documentary footage of King George's coronation. Harrer tiptoes in, takes a seat behind the Dalai Lama. Both stare at the flickering images on the screen in silence. Then, with his back to Harrer, the Dalai Lama speaks in a low voice, heavy with sorrow.

DALAI LAMA
Do you think someday people will look at Tibet on a movie screen? And wonder what happened to us?

HARRER
I don't know.

The Dalai Lama turns to face Harrer. They exchange a look of profound mutual regard.

DALAI LAMA
Don't you have all the answers, Heinrig?

HARRER
No, Kundun. I don't.

EXT. FIELD OUTSIDE LHASA — DAY

A team of yaks pull an ancient plough, tilling dry earth from a field.

HARRER'S NARRATION accompanies this image.

HARRER (V.O.)
On the same field where Tibetans traditionally gather for

184

picnics, ground was cleared to build an air strip...so that a plane carrying three Chinese generals could land.

Nearby, Harrer and Aufschnaiter unload crates, pass out new rifles to the ragtag assemblage of SOLDIERS on a clearing beside the field. Many of the troops wear steel mesh armor and carry old muskets. Others are nomads and farmers with no experience of war whatsoever. They look lost and bewildered.

> HARRER (V.O.)
> Nearby, the Tibetan Army practices maneuvers. Some of the soldiers wear ancient mesh armor, they bring old muskets and spears as artillery...

At the head, Tsarong is huddled with TWO MILITARY INSTRUCTORS trying to bring the troops to attention.

> HARRER (V.O.)
> The spectacle of a peace-loving nation...vainly attempting to create a military...the fear of war on my friends' faces...
> *(pauses, hesitant)*
> This has struck such a deeply buried, personal chord.

CLOSE ON HARRER'S FACE as he carefully observes everything around him.

> HARRER (V.O.)
> Echoes of the aggressions of my own country, the will to overpower weaker peoples...shame me, deeply. I shudder to recall how once, long ago, I embraced the same beliefs. How at one time I was no different from these intolerant Chinese.

EXT. STAIRWAY AND COURTYARD OF POTALA — DAY

Monks dressed in ceremonial regalia perform lama dances. Every courtyard of the palace is teeming with anxious displays of religious fervor—prayer wheels spin, incense burns, mantras fill the silence.

> HARRER (V.O.)
> The Tibetans say an enemy is the greatest teacher, because
> only an enemy can help develop patience and compassion.
> They believe with rock-like faith that the power of their
> religion will protect them against the Chinese.

CLOSE ON towering, delicately crafted sculptures, made entirely of butter.
Depicting protector deities, they slowly melt in the sun.

> HARRER (V.O.)
> In preparation for the Generals' visit, sacred ceremonies are
> performed throughout Lhasa. Sculptures of deities have
> been carved with great care in butter. As the sun melts them,
> they become a reminder that nothing lasts.

EXT. AIR STRIP — DAY

The Tibetan national flag with its regal snow lions and blazing sun is raised
up a pole. On a flagpole beside it, the blood red Chinese flag with its cres-
cent shaped constellation of yellow stars begins its ascent.

> HARRER (V.O.)
> The rising star of the Cabinet, Minister Ngawang Jigme,
> made an offering of his own: to greet the Chinese generals,
> and lead them through Lhasa.

Down below, the Tibetan Army stands at rigid attention alongside the completed air strip. Ministers of the Cabinet in their brocade finery wait near
them. Ngawang stands under the flagpoles, watching the two flags rise
together. Harrer comes up beside Ngawang.

> HARRER
> Raising their flag is an honor they don't deserve, Ngawang.

Harrer is taken aback to hear how detached and cynical Ngawang's response is.

> NGAWANG
> When you are not strong enough to fight, you should
> embrace your enemy. With both arms around you, he
> cannot point a gun at you.
> (smiles thinly)
> Nothing in politics is a matter of honor, my friend.

Moments later, a faint BUZZ in the sky is heard. The Tibetans crane their necks. Soon, a plane drops like a hallucination on this ancient medieval land. Murmurs and cries of fear as the Soviet-built transport, with its red star, descends to the runway, skids, and bounces to a halt.

Harrer pushes his way through the onlookers and finds Aufschnaiter and

Pema. The two Austrians watch with a sickening sense of déjà vu as a ramp is pushed to the plane. The door opens and TWO CHINESE GENERALS step out in their drab green uniforms. They are greeted by Ngawang. The Tibetan Army pathetically remains at attention as the military band strikes up a tune.

> AUFSCHNAITER
> History repeats itself, even in Paradise.

EXT. JOKHANG — LATE DAY

With nervous Tibetans following them like the Pied Piper, Ngawang escorts the Generals on a tour of the city, haughtily pointing out sites of interest as they approach the Jokhang.

INT. JOKHANG — DAY

Inside the holiest of Tibetan temples, hundreds of monks in crimson robes CHANT fervently. The temple is lit only by butter lamps; the air thick with the smoke of incense. In the center of the temple, monk artists kneel on the floor, and with fixed concentration apply colored sand to an intricate Kalachakra *mandala*—a representation of the five-story palace of the deity Kalachakra. The *mandala*—and the Kalachakra initiation for which it is constructed—has special significance for world peace.

The Chinese Generals walk right through the center of the sand painting. The horrified monks are frozen. They all turn to see the reaction of the Dalai Lama seated on his high throne at the front of the Jokhang. He is the personification of equanimity as the Generals are brought forward for introductions. Neither of the Generals bow. Neither offer scarves. Instead, they turn to Ngawang, scowling at the pillows placed on the ground for them.

> GENERAL CHANG JING-WU
> We do not sit lower than he does.

                    NGAWANG
General Chang Jing-wu, it is our custom . . .

                    DALAI LAMA
I can sit down there.

The hundreds of chanting monks cannot believe what comes next. The
Dalai Lama rises from his throne and descends the steps. He takes a seat
on a pillow across from the Generals. Ngawang crouches low to offer
introductions.

                    NGAWANG
     Your Holiness, this is General Chang Jing-wu, and General
     Than Gua-san. They have requested an audience with you.

The Dalai Lama folds his hands and bows his head.

                    DALAI LAMA
May you have happiness and prosperity.

EXT. JOKHANG — LATE DAY

Harrer, Aufschnaiter, and Pema are waiting with a throng of people,
pressed close to the massive temple doors. The doors open and a MONK
OFFICIAL pokes out his head to keep them apprised.

                    MONK OFFICIAL
     They're promising regional autonomy and religious freedom
     if Tibet agrees to let China be its political master.

INT. JOKHANG — LATE DAY

Now it is the Dalai Lama's turn to speak. He is very clear, completely at
ease with the Generals.

                    DALAI LAMA
Until I attain my majority, the Regent is the political leader

of Tibet. You should have requested an audience with him to discuss these important matters of the world. My experience of such things is limited.
                    (modestly)
I am a simple Buddhist monk. All I know is scripture and the words of Lord Buddha. He said: "All beings tremble before danger and death. Life is dear to all. When a man considers this, he does not kill or cause to kill." You must understand, these words are ingrained in the heart of every Tibetan. It is why we are a peaceful people, who reject violence on principle.
                    (smiles)
I pray you will see this is our great strength, not our weakness.

The Generals are floored.

DALAI LAMA
I thank you for your visit.

He reaches down to a bowl of *tsampa*—barley flour. Takes a pinch between two fingers and throws it into the air.

DALAI LAMA
An offering to the Enlightened Ones.

He signals for them to follow suit. Both Generals take a pinch of *tsampa* and disdainfully pitch it to the floor.

EXT. JOKHANG — DUSK

The massive doors are thrust open. Harrer, Pema, Aufschnaiter, and the crowd outside have to lunge backward as General Chang Jing-wu and Than Gua-san storm out of the temple.

GENERAL CHANG JING-WU
    Religion is poison.

Behind them, Ngawang leaves the temple, catching the eye of Harrer who is too heartsick to return his gaze.

EXT. ROOF OF POTALA — DUSK

Peering through his telescope, the Dalai Lama watches the Soviet transport plane circle Lhasa like a vulture, then turn toward the mountains and disappear beyond the ridges. The Dalai Lama sweeps the telescope around, traveling across the entire city of Lhasa. Almost trance-like, he mutters something under his breath. It takes a moment to realize he's saying a prayer.

EXT. TSARONG'S GARDEN — DAY

Tsarong dozes in a lounge chair. Tashi sets the table for lunch; nearby, Harrer repairs a broken umbrella. Both are silent, savoring this rare moment of calm. They are so preoccupied they don't see a weary MILITARY INSTRUCTOR enter the garden and take a seat next to Tsarong. The instructor lightly taps Tsarong's shoulder, waking him. Whispers in his ear.

> TSARONG
> *(loudly)*
>
> No.

Harrer's and Tashi's heads jerk up. Instinctively, Harrer goes straight to Tsarong. Tsarong hands him a wired message. Harrer reads it aloud.

> HARRER
> "Today at dawn, 84,000 troops of the First and Second Field Armies, under the overall command of General Chang Jing-wu, attacked the Tibetan frontier near Denkong. The Tibetan Army believes an attack on Chamdo, the capital of the eastern Tibetan province of Kham, is imminent..."

EXT. ROAD OUTSIDE CHAMDO FORT

An ancient stone fort sits high on a hill, protecting the city of Chamdo. A title comes up: CHAMDO, KHAM REGION — NEAR CHINESE BORDER.

HARRER'S VOICE continues reading the telegram.

> HARRER (V.O.)
> "Ngawang Jigme, our newly appointed governor there, is preparing to send troops toward the Chinese column in order to stop their progression."

INT. TIBETAN ARMY HEADQUARTERS IN CHAMDO — DAY

Proud and imperious, Ngawang Jigme stands by a window, staring out at

POV — THROUGH WINDOW:

The hustle of movement in the Chamdo Fort.

EXT. CHAMDO FORT — DAY

Inside the walls of fort, a large hillock at the center—an ammunition dump. A tunnel has been dug into the hillock; KHAMPAS haul guns, cannons, gunpowder down the tunnel into the dump. Troops of TIBETAN SOLDIERS march in sloppy, disorganized formation out the main gate.

INT. TIBETAN ARMY HEADQUARTERS — DAY

Still staring out the window, Ngawang Jigme is approached by MUJA DAGON, a straight-shooting, capable Tibetan General. Muja Dagon studies Ngawang a moment before speaking.

MUJA DAGON

As you're well aware, Ngawang Jigme, Chamdo is the gateway to Tibet. If Chamdo falls, the whole of Tibet will fall.

NGAWANG
(annoyed)

If I did not know that, I would not have been appointed Governor.

MUJA DAGON

I hope you also know, the troops will not accept surrender. They are committed to fighting the Chinese to the last man.

Ngawang turns to face the General, aware that he has been gently threatened.

NGAWANG

Rest assured, there will be no surrender as long as I am in Chamdo.

He turns to look out the window again and sees his own reflection in the glass.

EXT. CANYON — DUSK

In a well-protected canyon, exhausted Tibetan soldiers stop to make camp, setting loose their ponies to drink water from a nearby pond. CLOSE ON: The weary anxiety in the soldiers' eyes. CLOSE ON: The antiquated weapons, shoddy uniforms. Many wear torn robes of nomadic tribesmen.

EXT. RIDGE — DUSK

An endless line of CHINESE SOLDIERS marching at a jog, like a fast-flowing river of human bodies. CLOSE ON: their shiny new weapons and uniforms. CLOSE ON: the hardened set of their eyes.

EXT. CANYON — NIGHT

Tibetan troops sleep, their ponies resting beside the pond. Through the inky darkness, the endless file of Chinese troops fans out and slowly creeps toward the camp with deadly precision. A CHINESE COMMANDER silently gives the order to stop. In each SOLDIER'S hand a grenade is tightly clutched.

THE TIBETAN TROOPS: Almost all of the sleeping soldiers clasp strings of prayer beads in their hands. A YOUNG SERGEANT wakes up, hears the ponies WHINNEY in fear, can't see anything in the velvet blackness. Panicking, he rouses several MEN next to him. They HEAR more ominous sounds in the dark, quickly awaken all the troops sleeping nearby. Now, the SOUNDS of FOOTSTEPS seem to surround them on all sides; each soldier grips his rifle with a sense of desperate futility, not knowing where to aim.

Suddenly, the blackness explodes with piercing white light—FLARES are tossed from the summit, illuminating and exposing the terrified Tibetans.

GRENADES and MORTAR SHELLS hurl through the air. And the canyon erupts in violence. Soldiers are blown to pieces like rag dolls; the survivors scramble out in shock. Are taken down in a FUSILLADE of ARTILLARY FIRE.

THE CHINESE TROOPS: light more flares; toss them. And keep FIRING. The canyon is lit up with STREAKING BANDS OF LIGHT chasing Tibetan troops. They drop like flies as the torrent of GUNFIRE rains down on them. One TIBETAN SOLDIER manages to run away, leaps on a horse, and flees in terror.

EXT. GATES OF CHAMDO FORT

The soldier who escaped the massacre bolting on horseback into the fort.

INT. TIBETAN ARMY HEADQUARTERS — DAWN

The Soldier watches Ngawang Jigme calmly addressing Muja Dagon and other military officers.

NGAWANG

Radio Lhasa. Now. We request permission to surrender.

Muja Dagon looks as if he's been clubbed in the head.

MUJA DAGON

But . . . you said there would be no surrender as long as you—

Ngawang waves a hand to dismiss him, much the same way he was dismissed by the Regent long ago. His tone is icy.

NGAWANG

I said Radio Lhasa. Permission to surrender. Now.

He turns and leaves the room.

INT. ROOM IN ARMY HEADQUARTERS — DAWN

The SHARP CRACK of GUNFIRE echoes outside. With eerie poise, Ngawang removes a gold earring from his ear. Pulls off his yellow silk robes and dons a gray uniform.

EXT. FORT COURTYARD — DAWN

Ngawang slips out the back entrance. Mounts his horse. Heading toward the entrance gates, he passes a MAN awaiting him in shadows, holding a flaming torch.

INT. AMMUNITION DUMP — DAWN

Seen from inside the ammunition dump tunnel, Ngawang gives the man with torch a signal. The man enters the tunnel and disappears. Ngawang gives his horse a sharp kick.

EXT. FORT — DAWN

Ngawang gallops out of the fort.

EXT. ROAD OUTSIDE CHAMDO — DAWN

Fleeing down a dirt road, Ngawang glances back as a MASSIVE EXPLOSION erupts in the center of the fort.

EXT. CHAMDO FORT — DAWN

The ammunition dump has been set on fire.

INT./EXT. CEREMONIAL CANOPY ON FIELD IN LHASA — DAY

CLOSE ON A PIECE OF PAPER: In Chinese script. WIDER to reveal the Chinese General Chang Jing-wu presenting the paper with an exultant flourish to an anguished Muja Dagon. Chang Jing-wu sits on one side of a table; beside him is Than Gua-san.

Hear TSARONG'S VOICE narrating over the scene.

> TSARONG (O.S.)
> We lost a war in eleven days, Heinrich. This surrender is our
> death sentence.

On the other side of table, beside Muja Dagon, sits Ngawang Jigme. He avoids looking at the questioning, bewildered faces of many Tibetans hovering outside the canopy.

> TSARONG (O.S.)
> And I'm afraid our friend Ngawang Jigme has issued it.

MOVING TO THE OUTSIDE OF CANOPY: Harrer, Aufschnaiter, and Pema stand next to Tsarong, observing the proceedings with despair. Tears course freely down Tsarong's cheeks as he watches Muja Dagon hold a pen above the sealed act of unconditional surrender. The Chinese Generals wait patiently, all the time in the world on their hands.

TSARONG

He abandoned Chamdo. Had them destroy the ammunition dump. Without weapons and ammunition, there was no hope for the troops who wanted to fight.

(grief-stricken)

Our guerrillas could have held the mountain passes for months, even years. It would have bought us time to make appeals for help to other nations. Now it's lost. They broke down the gates.

EXT. GATES OF LHASA — EVENING

Chinese jeeps roll up the road toward the gates, blaring the grating Chinese anthem "THE EAST IS RED" from loudspeakers. Reaching the gates, the jeeps are slowed down by an undulating river of bodies snaking out of the city gates. It is a mass exodus from Lhasa—Tibetans transport their belongings on yak caravans, others carry everything they own on their backs.

EXT. PLA HEADQUARTERS — DAY

Harrer walks by the old Chinese Mission which has been converted to PLA headquarters; a banner of Mao is draped from the roof. Harrer sees Ngawang Jigme staring out a window, his expression unreadable.

EXT. COURTYARD IN FRONT OF PLA HEADQUARTERS — DAY

Ngawang rushes out of the building, gesturing for Harrer to join him. Harrer slowly walks into the courtyard, regards Ngawang with silent contempt.

NGAWANG

Hello, my friend. It's good to see you.

Harrer does not reply. Ngawang becomes defensive under Harrer's censorious gaze.

NGAWANG

We did what was best for our country. For Tibet.

Harrer peers around, at all the Chinese soldiers wearing PLA jackets. He shakes his head, disgusted.

HARRER

You know, all the way to Lhasa, I kept seeing Tibetans wearing these jackets. And they'd say, "Chinese soldiers very nice. They give money, food. Very nice." Funny how something so harmless as a jacket could symbolize such a great lie.

He removes the jacket he's wearing, the same one Ngawang gave to him years before. Hands it to him. Ngawang recoils, appalled.

NGAWANG

After all these years, you still do not understand our ways. It is an unforgivable insult to return a gift.

Harrer pushes the jacket into Ngawang's hand.

HARRER

A man who betrays his own culture shouldn't preach about its customs.

Furious, he turns and walks away from Ngawang.

EXT. JOKHANG — DAY

Harrer squeezes through a mass of bodies, reaches the front of Jokhang, where Aufschnaiter and a group of Tibetans are lighting myriad butter lamps. In front of the temple, Pema reads from a parchment in her hand.

PEMA

—We pray that his Holiness the Dalai Lama will be granted the power to unify his people. We humbly ask the Tibetan Government to honor our request and let the Dalai Lama attain his political majority.

EXT. GROUNDS IN FRONT OF POTALA GATES — DAY

CLOSE ON POSTER—A horizontal strip of paper being placed on an outdoor altar. It reads: "GIVE THE DALAI LAMA THE POWER." CLOSE ON ANOTHER POSTER: With the same message, being set near a *chorten*. WIDER TO REVEAL Tibetans putting the posters up in sacred places.

INT. GLASS APARTMENT ON POTALA ROOF — DAY

In a glass apartment on roof, the Dalai Lama squats over what appears to be a pile of mechanical parts, deeply engrossed in a task. Strewn on the floor are a multitude of disassembled music boxes and a tool kit. With incredible dexterity, the Dalai Lama reassembles the music box with the painted mountain on the lid. Smiles when he raises the lid and the same familiar LULLABY drifts from it. He gives a start when he hears a door open, relaxes when he sees Harrer enter the apartment.

HARRER

You've got the whole palace in a panic, Your Holiness.

DALAI LAMA

I'm hiding from the world for a day.

HARRER

Difficult to hide in a glass house, no?

The Dalai Lama shrugs. He is so uncharacteristically forlorn, Harrer is taken aback. He sits down to listen to the LULLABY still wafting from the music box.

HARRER

It's the "Moonlight." By Debussy.

DALAI LAMA

(smiles)

What else? What else do you know about this song?

Knowing the Dalai Lama's stalling for time, Harrer shakes his head. Eventually the lullaby dies out. Harrer gently takes the box and sets it down.

HARRER

We should go back down, Kundun.

EXT. TSARONG'S HOUSE — DAY

His face rigid with sorrow, Tsarong clips every flower in his magnificent garden, leaving it a mass of jagged stalks.

EXT. ROAD OUTSIDE LHASA — DAY

More jeeps carting Chinese TROOPS roar up the dirt road leading to Lhasa, passing streams of Tibetans fleeing the city. Among the refugees, pick up Tsarong and Tashi riding horseback. Tsarong stoically does not look back; keeps moving forward, toward the mountains.

EXT. STREET BELOW POTALA — DUSK

CLOSE ON: Prayer wheels furiously spinning. WIDER TO REVEAL: Crowds of Tibetans circumambulating the Potala, making prostrations, chanting and wailing to ward off their fear.

INT. DALAI LAMA'S BEDROOM — DAY

With his back facing us, the Dalai Lama sits cross-legged in front of a statue of the Buddha. Head lowered, posture ramrod-straight.

REVERSE ANGLE — DALAI LAMA: He is meditating. Eyes half-closed, staring without seeing. Hands folded in a graceful mudra; an image of translucent serenity.

EXT. STABLE — DAY

Harrer purchases several mules and ponies.

INT. HARRER'S HOUSE — NIGHT

Five knapsacks are laid out on the floor. Harrer outfits each pack with a complete kit of equipment and food. He reaches into a basket and removes two pistols. Places them inside a knapsack.

INT. HALLWAY OF POTALA — DAY

Harrer walks down the hall with the Lord Chamberlain.

> LORD CHAMBERLAIN
> You are coming to the enthronement, Mister Harrer? It's next week.

Harrer nods distractedly. They reach the door to the Dalai Lama's bed chambers. The GUARDS outside the door let him in.

INT. WAITING ROOM OF BED CHAMBER — DAY

Harrer takes a seat and waits. His anxious gaze travels across the room, taking in familiar objects and images. Stops at a *thangka* depicting a mountain rising from an ocean, surrounded by four continents.

> DALAI LAMA (O.S.)
> Do I look like an . . . egghead?

The Dalai Lama stands in the doorway. He is wearing eyeglasses. Self consciously pushes them up the bridge of his nose, not yet comfortable with them.

HARRER
(smiles)
No. They suit you.

The Dalai Lama comes in, immediately aware of Harrer's acute anxiety. He sits down.

DALAI LAMA
We have a saying in Tibet. If the problem can be solved, there's no use worrying about it. If it can't be solved, worrying will do no good.
(quietly)
So stop worrying, Heinrich.

HARRER
I'm sorry, I can't.
(urgently)
You should leave Tibet, Kundun. Your life is at great risk if you stay here.

The Dalai Lama cocks his head, listening with detached curiosity.

HARRER
If you'll forgive my presumption, I've made all the arrangements to escort you out safely. We can leave after the enthronement ceremony. The Chinese would never expect you to go then.

The Dalai Lama carefully absorbs this, moved by Harrer's concern.

DALAI LAMA
How can I help people if I run away from them? What kind of leader would I be?

He has struck such a deep nerve, Harrer can't respond.

> DALAI LAMA

I have to stay here, Heinrig. Serving others is my path to liberation.

There's a pause before Harrer speaks.

> HARRER

Then I won't go either.

> DALAI LAMA

Why not?

> HARRER

Because you are my path to liberation.

He seeks to make eye contact with the Dalai Lama, but the Dalai Lama looks away.

> DALAI LAMA

The Buddha said, "Salvation does not come from the sight of me. It demands strenuous effort and practice. So work hard and seek your own salvation diligently."
> *(looks at Harrer)*
I am not your son. And I never thought of you as my father. You were much too informal with me for that.

Afraid he might lose the slender hold on his emotions, Harrer closes his eyes. The Dalai Lama pauses a moment before speaking again.

> DALAI LAMA

Do you ever think about him?

Too overwhelmed to speak, Harrer nods his head.

> HARRER

All the time. Every day.

DALAI LAMA

And what do you think about?

Harrer takes a deep breath, trying not to cry.

HARRER

It's not a conscious thought anymore, Kundun. He's just
always there.
(pauses)
He crossed Tibet with me. He came to Lhasa with me.
When I visit you, he's there beside me...
(pauses)
He's just always there. I don't even remember how I pictured
the world without him in it.

DALAI LAMA

Then you should go home and be his father.

HARRER

I know.

He looks at the Dalai Lama, tears streaming down his face. The Dalai Lama
just flashes a brilliant smile.

DALAI LAMA

You've finished your job with me.

Harrer sighs with gratitude. The Dalai Lama impulsively takes Harrer's
hand in his.

DALAI LAMA

But you have to stay for my enthronement. I want you to see
me in all my pomp and glory.

HARRER

It would be a pleasure, my friend.

They sit there holding hands for a few moments.

                         DALAI LAMA
     Will you do me another favor?

                         HARRER
     Anything.

                         DALAI LAMA
     There's something I want to see before I become temporal
     leader of my country...

INT. MOVIE THEATRE AT POTALA — DAY

On screen, grainy black-and-white footage of scantily clad FEMALE
DANCERS bursting out of eggs and kicking their heels like frantic Chicken
Rockettes. Harrer and the Dalai Lama are convulsed in laughter as they
watch the film.

INT. DALAI LAMA'S BED CHAMBERS — PRE-DAWN

While darkness still hangs, the Dalai Lama stands with arms outstretched
as the Master of Robes wraps a green silk cloth around the waist of his ceremonial robes. A yellow silk cap rising to a curved point at top is gently
placed on his head.

The resonant, LOW DRONE of HORNS cuts the silence. Becoming louder...

INT. POTALA — HALL OF ALL GOOD DEEDS — DAY

HORNS, CYMBALS, and DRUMS rise to a crescendo. Seated on the vast, jewel-
encrusted Lion Throne, the Dalai Lama is a figure of regal poise. He
accepts the formal presentation of the GOLDEN WHEEL—a sacred, sculp-
tural object of solid gold—in the shape of a flame with an eight-spoked
wheel at its center. A humbled Regent presents the Golden Wheel.

REGENT

From the Tibetan government to Your Holiness the Fourteenth Dalai Lama.

(*pauses*)

We ask that you rule your people as spiritual and temporal leader of Tibet...

Taking the Golden Wheel in his hands, the Dalai Lama bows his head.

DALAI LAMA

By your prayers and wishes, I humbly accept.

Harrer sits in back of the Great Hall; innocuous and hidden in the midst of the fairy tale splendor of the ceremony. As everyone rises to bow and

prostrate, Harrer rises, too. With the fluid grace of a seasoned practitioner, he performs three prostrations, expressing his devotion to the new leader of Tibet.

INT. AUFSCHNAITER'S HOUSE — DAY

CLOSE ON A CUP OF BUTTER TEA being poured. A thick coat of butter rises to the surface. Aufschnaiter hands the cup to Harrer. Harrer gulps it down quickly, makes a face.

> HARRER
> Butter tea was never my cup of tea.

He sets the cup down. Aufschnaiter quickly refills it.

> HARRER
> Thank you. But one was enough.

> AUFSCHNAITER
> Follow the customs. A fresh cup of tea is poured for the
> loved one departing...

Harrer groans and hefts the cup but is stopped midway. Aufschnaiter takes the cup of tea from Harrer's hand and sets it on the table.

> AUFSCHNAITER
> It sits untouched, waiting for his return.

EXT. AUFSCHNAITER'S HOUSE — DUSK

Pema and Aufschnaiter on their porch watch Harrer retreat down the road with a bulging knapsack on his back.

INT. AUFSCHNAITER'S HOUSE — DUSK

The cup of tea sits on the table, full to the brim.

EXT. POTALA — DAY

Harrer climbs the long flight of stairs to the palace, peering out at

POV — LHASA: Shining like a jewel.

EXT. POTALA STAIRCASE — DAY

HARRER keeps climbing the steps until he reaches the wide courtyard at the top.

EXT. COURTYARD — DAY

The Dalai Lama is waiting for him; his crimson monk's robe billows in the breeze. At a mere fourteen years old, he has quickly assumed the demeanor of a mature leader and man. He steps forward to greet Harrer. The two friends silently regard each other with abiding tenderness and love. Then, the Dalai Lama does something he's never done before with Harrer.

He blesses him.

Pressing his forehead to Harrer's, he holds it there as he recites a prayer.

> DALAI LAMA
> "May all travelers find happiness everywhere they go. Without any effort may they accomplish whatever they set out to do. And having safely returned to the shore, may they be joyfully reunited with their relatives."

Then he gently places a *khata* around Harrer's neck.

EXT. STAIRCASE OF POTALA — DAY

From a distance, see Harrer descending the staircase. At the bottom, a MONK ATTENDANT waits for him, hands him a small package wrapped in brown paper.

MONK ATTENDANT
   From His Holiness.

EXT. LHASA GATE — DAY

Passing more Chinese jeeps hurtling toward Lhasa, Harrer leaves the city on the same road from which he entered many years ago. He slows his pace, aware of the crystalline light shifting across the lush Kyichu valley, the rich sounds of CHIMES and CHANTING in the distance. He stops. Slowly turns back to face Lhasa. Lifts his gaze upward to the Potala and smiles.

POV — POTALA:

A small figure is perched at the edge of the roof, peering through a telescope.

EXT. STREET IN AUSTRIA — DAY

A title appears: AUSTRIA, 1951. A bus with an advertisement for vacuum cleaners on its side roars down a busy street, screeches to a stop at a kiosk. Men and women rush like maniacs to catch the bus, screaming. Among the crowds on the street, pick up Harrer walking slowly, carrying a small package wrapped in brown paper. He reaches the entrance to an elegant apartment building. Scans the names on the buzzer. Pauses before pressing one.

INT. APARTMENT DOORWAY — DAY

An apartment door opens. Behind it stands Ingrid; a few feet behind her is Horst. Both are gripped with self-consciousness as Harrer lingers in the doorway, waiting to be asked in.

                    INGRID
        I told him you were coming.

She steps aside to let Harrer enter the apartment. He and Horst nod a greeting to one another. No one knows what to say.

INT. APARTMENT LIVING ROOM — DAY

Harrer follows Ingrid through the spacious, well-appointed living room. She leads him down a hallway.

INT. HALLWAY — DAY

Ingrid stops outside a closed door. Taps lightly on it, then opens it.

> INGRID
> Rolf? Come out and meet...him.

A BOY'S VOICE calls out from inside.

> ROLF (O.S.)
> I don't want to.

She glances back at Harrer, who gamely shrugs. Then he politely gestures for her to step aside. And he walks into the bedroom.

INT. BEDROOM — DAY

Every imaginable kind of shiny new toy and athletic trophy is proudly displayed on the shelves in the room. Harrer seems overwhelmed by the abundance of possessions an eleven-year-old boy can have. But there is no boy anywhere.

Harrer spots a closet door, opened a crack. Smiles to himself. Sets the package on a table and slowly unwraps it. Harrer covertly glances over to see the closet door opening a bit wider.

He removes the gift from the wrapping paper. It is the MUSIC BOX with the painted image of the mountain on lid. The closet door is half open and a shimmer of blond hair can be seen in the gap.

With infinite patience, Harrer winds the key to the music box. The closet door remains closed. He gently opens the box's lid and the DEBUSSY

LULLABY fills the room. Then he places the box outside the closet door and quietly leaves the bedroom.

INT. HALLWAY — DAY

Harrer peers through a crack in the bedroom door, watches as

POV — IN BEDROOM

The closet door slowly opens. Like a dreamer lured by a siren's song, ROLF HARRER emerges from the closet. He is a miniature mirror image of Harrer. He looks all around to make sure Harrer isn't there, then leans down and puts his ear to the music box, utterly enchanted.

INT. HALLWAY — DAY

Quietly content, Harrer watches his son, then slowly makes his way down the hall.

EXT. ROCK FACE — DAY

A TITLE APPEARS: 1959.

An older Harrer belays Rolf up a rock wall, to the top. When Rolf joins him at the summit, father and son exchange looks of admiration.

A SCROLL appears over the image of Harrer sitting on the ridge, Rolf a distance away. Planted next to Harrer is a small flag. CLOSER ON FLAG: The tiny cloth snaps in the wind, revealing the white snow lions of the Tibetan national flag.

SCROLL:

Over 1.2 million Tibetans have died as a result of the Chinese occupation of Tibet. Over six thousand monasteries were destroyed.

In 1959, the Dalai Lama was forced to flee to India. He still lives there today, trying to promote a peaceful resolution with the Chinese.

After returning to Austria, Heinrich Harrer wrote Seven Years in Tibet *and several other books about the tolerant people and spiritual culture which so deeply affected him.*

In 1989, the Dalai Lama was awarded the Nobel Peace Prize.

Heinrich Harrer and the Dalai Lama remain friends to this day.

THE END

This is the last photograph that Heinrich Harrer took as he was leaving Lhasa. As he recalled, "I left Lhasa in mid-November 1950 as the Chinese invasion intensified. It was with a heavy heart that I left my beloved home and garden and my servants who stood around me weeping. The sky was overcast when I embarked in my little yak-hide boat that was to take me down the Kyichu River to its confluence with the Tsangpo. Floating down the river, I could not keep my eyes off the Potala—I knew the Dalai Lama was on the roof watching my departure through his telescope."

Screening the Truth about Tibet

by Robert A. F. Thurman

Jey Tsong Khapa Professor of Indo-Tibetan Buddhist Studies, Columbia University

I was so moved by this beautiful film, I must pay homage to all the people who created it. For the first time in a major motion picture, the general public can glimpse the true story of the Tibetan holocaust.

Screenwriter Becky Johnston skillfully portrayed the epic tale of a champion mountain-climber failing to conquer the high Himalayas, and then escaping the nightmare of world war into a real Shangri-la more amazing than the fiction. She also revealed the more important quest within the hero's heart, wherein his encounter with the young Dalai Lama and the Tibetan people enabled him to discover his own humanity. Brad Pitt courageously chose to portray a difficult character going through a sustained ordeal, finding himself, and becoming the champion of a special people in mortal danger.

Jean-Jacques Annaud understood the profundity of a Tibetan culture that could change the heart of a man from the West, and rose to the challenge of telling this historic adventure. He began with a wanderer seeking himself in the most exotic of all lands, and ended with the story of a unique people with a unique leader. Abandoned by the world for fifty years, they have kept their humanity while struggling for their lives during invasion, colonization, cultural deprivation, and a genocide that continues to this day.

Heinrich Harrer was one of the handful of Europeans who lived in the old Tibet during the years just before its devastation. He became perfectly fluent in the language, expert in the elegant Tibetan spoken in Lhasa. Though he developed a great appreciation for the Tibetan people and their way of life, he did not delve deeply into the central focus of their highly developed culture: Buddhism, with its philosophies, arts, ceremonies, yogas, and sophisticated ethics. Thus, when he raised his cry about the fate of Tibet to the uncaring world through his famous book and his tireless lecturing, his concern for the Tibetans was all the more powerful, coming from a European who had not "gone native."

China invaded Tibet in 1949 and 1950, under the false pretext that Tibet was its possession, to be "liberated from imperialists." Tibet had never been conquered and, though isolated, had always been independent—even in modern terms—since 1912. This, in fact, was well known to England, Russia, Nationalist China, and America. The permanent population of Chinese in Tibet's mostly three-mile-high territory was exactly zero, and the "imperialists" amounted to less than a handful of Western visitors.

Over the next thirty years, the Communists divided up Tibet into one so-called Autonomous Region (home to only one-third of all Tibetans), one separate province (Qinghai), and four autonomous prefectures of other Chinese provinces. They killed more than 1.2 million of the 6 million Tibetans. They destroyed 6,254 major monastic towns, leaving only thirteen partially standing, though desecrated. They forced all 800,000 monks and nuns to disrobe, denounce religion, or kill each other at gunpoint; only a few thousand succeeded in fleeing over Himalayan passes to sanctuary in exile in Nepal, Bhutan, or India. They imprisoned hundreds of thousands of Tibetans—all the upper classes and many of the lower classes supposedly to be liberated—for clinging to Buddhism and resisting the Maoist barrel-of-a-gun ideology. And they began the process of colonizing Tibet with Chinese settlers: encouraging intermarriage, forcing sterilization on Tibetan women, preventing Tibetans from learning their own language, taking children from their homes by force for schooling in China, and so on.

From the very beginning, it was Chinese government policy to ratify their naked seizure of Tibet by genocide of Tibetan people and destruction of Tibetan culture and material civilization, replacing it with Chinese people, communist "culture," and the modern, homogeneous, concrete Chinese city. In 1950, Mao vowed publicly that he would settle 50 million Chinese in Tibet by 1960. In the Tibet working committee meeting in 1994, Li Peng's cadres vowed that the "Tibetan problem" would be solved at last by intensive economic development, requiring millions more Chinese to move in on a priority basis. This is a clear case of the genocide of one people by another, going on right now.

The main reason this genocide has not already been completed, despite China's massive human resources and years of effort, and the ignorance or hypocritical apathy of the rest of the world, is Tibet's unique geography. Its land averages 15,000 feet high, and Chinese farming cannot support any sizable populations in such a climate. The Chinese colonists live mainly in army compounds, work camps, or artificial, newly constructed cities, supplied with everything by air or by 2,000-mile truck routes on constantly collapsing mountain roads. They have recovered the enormous subsidies paid to lure them into this high-altitude discomfort by raping Tibet's resources: clear-cutting 75 percent of her primeval forests, strip-harvesting her uniquely potent Himalayan medicinal herbs, killing 90 percent of her wildlife, extracting her minerals with ecologically devastating methods, overgrazing and desertifying her fragile high-altitude steppes, and producing hydroelectric power by draining pristine glacial lakes and disrupting silting patterns of powerful mountain rivers.

What very few realize about Tibet is that this genocide will inevitably fail. If the Chinese could replace Tibetans, who have adapted to their unique environment over millennia, they would have done so long ago: Tibet's million-square-mile area would have been populated by 50 million people for centuries. No small clique of dictators will be inclined to spend the hundreds of billions required to prop up artificial settlements forever. So, when geopolitical posturing has become unnecessary in a global world, when Tibet's resources have been totally depleted, the Chinese settlers will go back home anyway. Then the world will witness the tragedy of the surviving Tibetans re-emerging in a daze, their once beautiful country an utter wasteland.

The full impact of this disaster can be avoided now if the people of the world, including the people of China, see what is happening. When they really see it, they will insist that the confused, short-sighted leaders (not only of China but of all the countries involved) change their immoral, uneconomical policies.

Seven Years in Tibet subtly but unflinchingly tells the truth about Tibet and its appalling tragedy. It is a gripping human drama, and its truth can make us free. The 1989 Nobel Peace Prize laureate, His Holiness the Dalai Lama, has said, "Our only weapon is the truth." Only truth can free the Tibetans. Only truth can free the Chinese. All of us are bound to their tragedy, whether we know it or not. So we all need this truth.

FURTHER READING

Avedon, John. *In Exile from the Land of Snows*, Harper Perennial, 1994.

———. *An Interview with the Dalai Lama*, Little Bird Publications, 1980.

Batchelor, Stephen. *Tibet Guide*, Wisdom Publications, 1987.

Bell, Charles. *The Portrait of the Dalai Lama*, Wisdom Publications, 1987.

Chan, Victor. *Tibet Handbook*, Moon Publications, 1994.

Coleman, Graham. *A Handbook of Tibetan Culture*, Shambala, 1994.

Dalai Lama, *The Fourteenth. Freedom in Exile*, Harper Collins, 1991.

———. *My Land and My People*, McGraw-Hill, 1962.

———. *Kindness, Clarity and Insight*, Snow Lion Publications, 1985.

———. *A Policy of Kindness*, Snow Lion Publications, 1993.

———. *The World of Tibetan Buddhism*, Wisdom, 1995.

David-Neel, Alexandra. *My Journey to Lhasa*, Beacon Press, 1993.

———. *Mystery and Magic in Tibet*, Dover, 1971.

Ford, Robert. *Captured in Tibet*, George Harrap & Co., 1957.

Goldstein, Melvyn. *History of Modern Tibet 1913-1951*, University of California Press, 1989.

Goodman, Michael Harris. *The Last Dalai Lama*, Shambala, 1986.

Govinda, Lama Anagarika. *The Way of the White Clouds*, Ms. Rider and Co., 1993.

———. *The Foundations of Tibetan Mysticism*, Samuel Weiser, 1991.

Harrer, Heinrich. *Seven Years in Tibet*, Tarcher/Putnam, 1981.

———. *Return to Tibet*, Penguin, 1985.

———. *Lost Lhasa*, Abrams/Summit, 1992.

Lhalungpa, Lobsang. *Tibet: Sacred Realm, Photographs 1880-1950*, Time Books International, 1983.

Normanton, Simon. *Tibet, the Lost Civilization*, Viking, 1989.

Peissel, Michel. *Cavaliers of Kham: the Secret War in Tibet*, William Heinemann, 1972.

Richardson, Hugh. *Short History of Tibet*, E. P. Dutton, 1962.

—————. *Ceremonies of the Lhasa Year*, Serindia Publications, 1993.

Rowell, Galen and the Dalai Lama. *My Tibet*, University of California Press, 1995.

Shantideva. *A Guide to the Bodhisattva's Way of Life*. Translated by Stephen Batchelor. Library of Tibetan Works and Archives, 1979, 1992.

Snellgrove, David and Hugh Richardson. *A Cultural History of Tibet*, Weidenfeld & Nicholson, 1968.

Sogyal, Rimpoche. *The Tibetan Book of Living and Dying*, Harpers San Francisco, 1994.

Taring, Rinchen Dolma. *Daughter of Tibet*, Wisdom, 1986.

Thomas, Lowell. *Silent War in Tibet*, Doubleday & Co., 1959.

Thurman, Robert. Editor and translator. *Tibetan Book of the Dead*, Bantam Book, 1994.

Tucci, Giuseppe. *To Lhasa and Beyond*, Snow Lion Publications, 1983.

Tung, Rosemary Jones. *A Portrait of Lost Tibet*, Snow Lion Publications, 1987.

MANDALAY ENTERTAINMENT *presents*
A Repérage *and* Vanguard Films/Applecross Production
A film by Jean-Jacques Annaud

Brad Pitt

SEVEN YEARS IN TIBET

David Thewlis
B. D. Wong
Mako
Jamyang Jamtsho Wangchuk
Lhakpa Tsamchoe
Jetsun Pema

Music by John Williams
Cello Solos by Yo-Yo Ma
Costumes Designed by Enrico Sabbatini
Director of Photography Robert Fraisse
Executive Producers   Richard Goodwin   Michael Besman   David Nichols
Produced by   Jean-Jacques Annaud   John H. Williams   Iain Smith
Based on the book by Heinrich Harrer
Screenplay by Becky Johnston
Directed by Jean-Jacques Annaud

A TriStar Pictures Release, U.S., Canada, Australia & New Zealand
An Entertainment Film Distributors Release, United Kingdom

ABOUT THE AUTHORS

After graduating from the prestigious L'Institut des Hautes Etude Ciné-matographiques at the age of twenty, JEAN-JACQUES ANNAUD quickly achieved success directing commercials. When he was twenty-three, his career was inter-rupted by National Service which, for him, meant being sent to the French Cameroons as an Army Film Director. There he trained the local people to make their own movies and he made a series of educational films. He fell in love with Africa and decided that his first feature film would be made there.

Having decided not to continue with commercials, Annaud set out to make the feature film he had promised himself, *Black and White in Color*, which won the Oscar for Best Foreign Language Film in 1978. He directed the comedy *Coup de Tête*, from a screenplay by Francis Verber, the author of *La Cage Aux Folles*. He then went on to direct *Quest for Fire*, *The Name of the Rose*, and *The Bear*, all of which won César Awards. *The Lover* and the 3-D IMAX film *Wings of Courage* followed.

BECKY JOHNSTON was born in Michigan and trained as a fine arts painter at Rhode Island School of Design and Brown University. Her desire to write films led her to move to Los Angeles, where she spent as much time she could at the American Film Institute Library, teaching herself to write scripts. Her first pro-duced script was for the Prince feature *Under The Cherry Moon*, and in 1991 she received an Academy Award nomination for her screenplay for *The Prince of Tides*, which starred Barbra Streisand. She has recently finished the script for a new version of *Laura*, and has embarked on another project with director Jean-Jacques Annaud.

LAURENCE CHOLLET is a freelance writer based in the New York area. His work has appeared in numerous publications, including the *Los Angeles Times*, the *Los Angeles Times Magazine*, *The Manchester Guardian*, the *Shambala Sun*, and *Projections*. He is currently working on a book about Annaud and his films.

ACKNOWLEDGMENTS

Permission to reprint copyrighted material from the following sources is gratefully acknowledged:

Map reprinted from *Seven Years in Tibet*, by Heinrich Harrer. By permission of Jeremy Tarcher Books. (Pages 6–7.)

Photographs by Heinrich Harrer used by permission of Heinrich Harrer. (As credited on pages 8, 19, 24, 26, 32, 48, 51, 70, 215.) Some of these photographs have appeared previously in *Seven Years in Tibet* (Tarcher/Putnam, 1981) and in *Lost Lhasa* (Abrams/Summit, 1992).

Photographs by Jean-Jacques Annaud used by permission of Jean-Jacques Annaud. (Starting after page 63 in the "Portfolio of Images.")

Laurence Chollet would like to thank Jean-Jacques Annaud, for making all of this possible; Alisa Tager, Robert Fraisse, Becky Johnston, Enrico Sabbatini, Susan d'Arcy, and Laurence Annaud, for patiently bearing with endless questions to give invaluable help; and Gerard Fataboy Rauluk, Anne Moore, and Betsy Chollet, for providing "editorial assistance."

The publisher wishes to thank the following for their generous help:

At Mandalay Entertainment: John Jacobs, Darrell Walker, Dennis Nollette, Fae Horowitz, Zayda Vidal, Paul Goldsmith, Susan d'Arcy, and Melanie Hodal and Kimberly Richards-Wire at DDA.

At Seven Years in Tibet, Los Angeles office: Stacy Arnold.

At High Plateau Productions: Michael Saxton and Giulia Maura.

At Repérage: Véronique Bataille.

At the Heinrich Harrer Project: Leslie diRusso

At the Marsh Agency: Susanna Nicklin

At Walking Stick Press: Linda Herman, Diana Landau, Miriam Lewis, and Joanna Lynch.

Soundtrack composed by John Williams and featuring Yo-Yo Ma. Available on CD.

I.

2.

3.

4.

5.

7.

8.

10.

II.

13.

14.

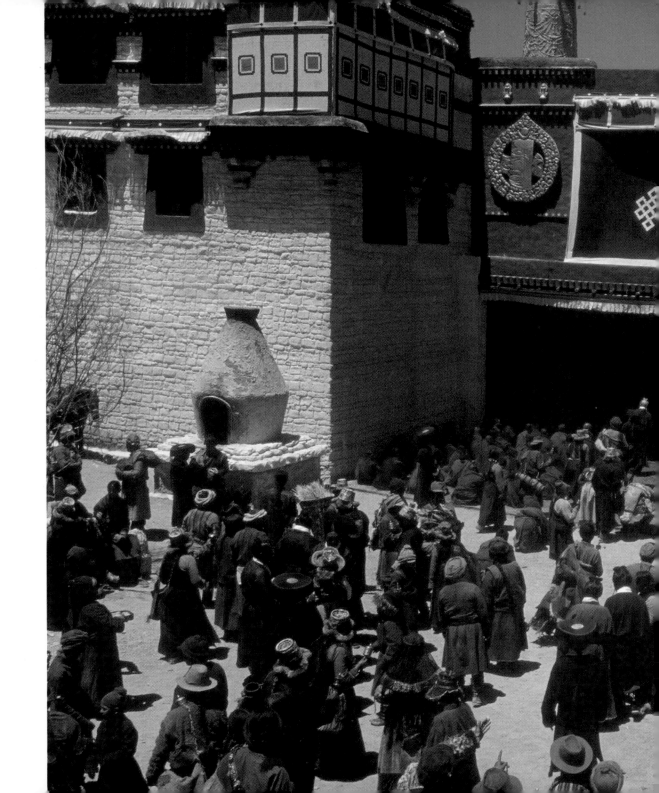

16.

17.

18.

19.

20.

21.

23.